$16.9

WORLD BANK STAFF OCCASIONAL PAPERS □ NUMBER THIRTY-ONE

Mahmood Ali Ayub

Made in Jamaica
The Development of the
Manufacturing Sector

Published for the World Bank
The Johns Hopkins University Press
Baltimore and London

The Johns Hopkins University Press
Baltimore, Maryland 21218, U.S.A.

Copyright © 1981 by The International Bank
for Reconstruction and Development / THE WORLD BANK
1818 H Street, N.W., Washington, D.C. 20433, U.S.A.
Manufactured in the United States of America

Library of Congress Cataloging in Publication Data
Ayub, Mahmood Ali, 1948–
  Made in Jamaica.
  (World Bank staff occasional paper; no. 31)
  Bibliography: p. 125
  1. Jamaica—Manufactures. 2. Jamaica—Industries.
I. Title. II. Series: World Bank staff occasional
papers; no. 31.
HD9734.J32A98   338.4'7'00097292   80-27765
ISBN 0-8018-2568-7 (pbk.)

Contents

TABLES

Foreword

••

I would like to explain why the World Bank does research work and why this research is published. We feel an obligation to look beyond the projects that we help finance toward the whole resource allocation of an economy and the effectiveness of the use of those resources. Our major concern, in dealings with member countries, is that all scarce resources— including capital, skilled labor, enterprise, and know-how— should be used to their best advantage. We want to see policies that encourage appropriate increases in the supply of savings, whether domestic or international. Finally, we are required by our Articles, as well as by inclination, to use objective economic criteria in all our judgments.

These are our preoccupations, and these, one way or another, are the subjects of most of our research work. Clearly, they are also the proper concern of anyone who is interested in promoting development, and so we seek to make our research papers widely available. In doing so, we have to take the risk of being misunderstood. Although these studies are published by the Bank, the views expressed and the methods explored should not necessarily be considered to represent the Bank's views or policies. Rather, they are offered as a modest contribution to the great discussion on how to advance the economic development of the underdeveloped world.

ROBERT S. MCNAMARA
President
The World Bank

Preface

•-•··•··•··•-•·•·

This study draws on my experience as a country economist for Jamaica in the World Bank from 1977 to 1979. On
various occasions during that time the work of Bank staff was
impeded by lack of qualitative and quantitative information on
key aspects of the manufacturing sector in Jamaica. This scarcity
of information assumed operational significance when the Bank
became involved in the Small-Scale Enterprises Project and the
Second Program Loan, the latter loan requiring, among other
conditions, policy changes in the industrial incentives in the
country. With encouragement from colleagues, particularly
John Holsen and Robert Kanchuger, and some prodding from
officials of the Ministry of Industry and Commerce in Jamaica, I
embarked upon this study of the major aspects and evolution of
Jamaica's manufacturing sector. Although the study focuses on
the Jamaican experience, the issues discussed have relevance for
the industrial sectors of many developing countries.

I would like to express my deep appreciation to Enrique
Lerdau for allowing me to extricate myself from operational
work for three months to concentrate on this study. I am also
indebted to Sidney E. Chernick for providing me an office and a
conducive environment to complete the research.

In preparing the revised version, I have benefited greatly from
detailed comments by Gladstone Bonnick, Donald Keesing,
Demetrious Papageorgiou, Guy Pfeffermann, Gary Pursell, and
Xavier Simon. Excellent programming and research assistance
was provided by Satish Manan and Anna Tsiakki. I am, of
course, responsible for all remaining shortcomings.

It would not have been possible to undertake this study without the active cooperation of the Jamaican government, the
private sector, and the students and staff of the University of

West Indies, Mona campus. In particular, the support of Rt. Hon. Danny Williams, then minister of industry and commerce, and the advice of Roderick Rainford proved invaluable. The industrial survey, on which much of this study is based, was carried out under the guidance of A.B. and M.E. Associates and Jamaica Manufacturers Association, and was financed by Jamaica Export Credit Insurance Corporation. Ahmed Zia Mian, an economist with the United Nations Development Programme (UNDP) in Kingston, made many helpful comments. I am grateful to all these individuals and organizations.

My thanks also go to Iliana Brown and Antonieta Polo who ably typed the successive versions of this study.

Virginia deHaven Hitchcock edited the final manuscript for publication. Brian J. Svikhart supervised production of the book, Harry Einhorn read and corrected proof, and Raphael Blow prepared the figure.

MAHMOOD ALI AYUB

Definitions

•─•

ADA	Accelerated depreciation allowance
CARICOM	Caribbean Community
CARIFTA	Caribbean Free Trade Association
CIEL	Cement Industry Encouragement Law
c.i.f.	Cost, insurance, freight
DRC	Domestic resource cost
EEC	European Economic Community
EIEL	Export Industries Encouragement Law
EPC	Effective protection coefficient
ESC	Effective subsidy coefficient
f.o.b.	Freight on board
GDP	Gross domestic product
GSP	Generalized System of Preferences
IIL	Industrial Incentives Law
IMF	International Monetary Fund
JECIC	Jamaica Export Credit Insurance Corporation
JIDC	Jamaica Industrial Development Corporation
JMA	Jamaica Manufacturers' Association
JNEC	Jamaica National Export Corporation
NBER	National Bureau of Economic Research
NPC	Nominal protection coefficient
OECD	Organization for Economic Cooperation and Development
PIEL	Pioneer Industrial Encouragement Law
PRI	Preferential rate of interest
STC	State Trading Corporation
TICA	Tobacco Industries Control Authority
TIEL	Textile Industry Encouragement Law

Made in Jamaica
The Development of the Manufacturing Sector

1

•◦•

Introduction and Summary

One of the most striking features of the manufacturing sector of Jamaica is that it is relatively varied for a country of just over 2 million inhabitants. Although the initial impetus for industrial development came from the demands of the sugar and other food subsectors, the sector now produces a wide variety of manufactured products, from garments and processed foods to machinery and electrical equipment. Table 1-1 illustrates the gradual diversification that occurred in the sector, primarily in response to a vigorous policy of import substitution, despite the small size of the local market.

Not only did manufacturing become more diversified, the sector also grew in relation to the rest of the economy. In 1950 manufacturing accounted for 11.3 percent of gross domestic product (GDP), a share which increased steadily to 15.7 percent in 1970 and to 18.2 percent by 1977. By the latter year, manufacturing had become the largest sector in terms of its contribution to GDP, but in 1978, distributive trade once again regained the first place by a small margin (Table 1-2).

Growth rates in the sector have varied considerably, averaging about 7.6 percent annually in real terms during 1950–68, about 5.2 percent during 1969–73, and declining at an annual rate of 3.8 percent during 1974–78. The factors behind these variable rates are discussed in the next two chapters.

The sector employed about 79,000 persons in 1978, approximately 10 percent of the total employed labor force. It also provided about US$72 million (excluding sugar and petroleum products exports and re-exports) or about 10 percent of total merchandise exports in that year.

3

Table 1-1. *Composition of Value-Added*
in Selected Manufacturing Subsectors, 1950 to 1978
(percent)

Subsector	1950	1960	1970	1975	1978
Sugar, rum, and molasses	27.8	17.8	5.8	5.8	2.0
Other food, beverages, and tobacco	41.9	35.9	40.4	41.4	40.6
Textiles, footwear, and garments	8.2	9.0	7.4	8.3	7.4
Furniture, fixtures, and wood products	4.4	7.6	5.6	4.6	4.4
Printing, publishing, and paper products	2.2	6.0	4.1	5.9	4.5
Cement and clay products	0.3	6.8	5.6	4.3	3.1
Metal products	1.3	10.1	14.2	13.7	14.0
Chemicals	2.6	4.5	10.0	8.1	8.3
Other	11.3	2.3	6.9	7.9	15.7
Total	100.0	100.0	100.0	100.0	100.0

Source: Data for 1950, derived from Owen Jefferson, *The Post-War Economic Development of Jamaica* (Kingston, Jamaica: University of the West Indies, 1972); data for 1960–78, Department of Statistics.

Need for the Study

Despite its significance, the manufacturing sector has received almost no detailed analysis. Chernick's regional study provides useful insights, but its scope is much wider, dealing with all the sectors of all the Commonwealth Caribbean countries.[1] Chen-Young's study provides a useful data base, but the analysis is sketchy.[2] From time to time government and multilateral agencies have provided background material on the sector, but time constraints and the operational nature of the work have inhibited a detailed analysis.[3]

1. Sidney E. Chernick, *The Commonwealth Caribbean* (Baltimore: The Johns Hopkins University Press, 1978).
2. Paul Chen-Young and Associates, "Capacity Utilization and Export Potential in the Manufacturing Sector" (study prepared for JMA (Jamaican Manufacturers' Association), Jamaica, 1977; processed).
3. See, for example, National Planning Agency, "Green Paper on Industrial Development Program—Jamaica, 1975–1980" (Kingston, 1975); National Planning Agency, "Emergency Production Plan" (Kingston, 1977); World Bank, "Current Economic

Table 1-2. *Contribution of Sectors to* GDP
at Current Market Prices, 1950 to 1978
(percent)

Sector	1950	1960	1970	1975	1978
Agriculture[a]	} 30.8	12.1	6.7	7.6	8.5
Mining and quarrying		9.7	12.6	10.2	13.4
Manufacturing	11.3	14.0	15.7	16.7	16.9
Electricity and water	1.1	1.1	1.0	1.4	2.3
Construction and installation	7.6	11.9	13.3	9.5	6.6
Distributive trades	15.1	18.1	19.0	19.5	17.1
Transport and communication	7.1	7.8	5.5	6.0	6.0
Financial services	2.6	3.4	3.8	4.1	3.9
Real estate	5.8	3.1	9.4	9.5	8.6
Public administration	6.1	6.1	7.8	12.0	13.4
Other services	12.5	12.7	5.2	3.5	3.3
GDP at current market prices	100.0	100.0	100.0	100.0	100.0

a. Including fishery and forestry.
Source: Department of Statistics.

One significant constraint has been lack of comprehensive data on the sector. During the past few years, however, new dis-aggregated data have become available, partly as a by-product of the government's new concern for the development of the sector.

Purpose of the Study

This study aims to use available data and information and to provide new information that should help in a better understanding of the sector. It provides a reasonably comprehensive account of the key characteristics of the manufacturing sector in Jamaica and assesses the importance of various factors in determining the structure of the sector. Effort has been made to follow the evolution of the sector during the past two decades, to

Position and Prospects of Jamaica" (a restricted-circulation document) (Washington, D.C., May 1979); Inter-American Development Bank, "Socioeconomic Report—Jamaica," (Washington, D.C., July 1979; processed).

give a detailed picture of the extent of protection provided to the sector in 1978, and to examine the prospects for growth of manufacturing exports during the next several years. On the basis of this analysis, certain policy recommendations are made.

Sources and Biases of the Data

This study combines rigorous empirical analysis where feasible and more informal study, including a brief economic history of the sector. To that extent, portions of the study convey some of the untidiness and complexity of the real world. It uses both macro and micro data.

The main sources for macroeconomic data were the Department of Statistics, Bank of Jamaica, National Planning Agency, Ministry of Industry and Commerce, Ministry of Finance, Jamaica Manufacturers' Association (JMA), Jamaica Export Credit Insurance Corporation (JECIC), Jamaica National Export Corporation (JNEC), and the Trade Administrator's Department. The last three are compiling useful, disaggregated data, which should prove helpful in future work on the sector.

Most of this study is based on disaggregated microeconomic data. In theory, there are two sources for such data: either an input-output matrix or cost and production data obtained from a survey of firms. Clearly, if a reasonably comprehensive and up-to-date input-output table is available, it can save a great deal of time and effort.[4] Studies based on dated input-output tables can be quite misleading, however. Not only does protection change over time, but so do the techniques of production and the input mix. Large structural changes also may have occurred during the period. Yates has shown that input-output tables more than a decade old may impart sizable bias to the estimates of protection, even if there is little apparent effect on industry rankings.[5]

---

4. The National Planning Agency is preparing a new input-output table that is expected to be ready by early 1981.

5. A. J. Yates, "An Analysis of the Effect of Production Process Changes on Effective Protection Estimates," *Review of Economics and Statistics* (February 1976).

In the case of Jamaica, the latest input-output table is more than a decade old, which clearly is unsuitable in view of the large structural changes that have occurred in the economy since that time. Nor is that table comprehensive enough to provide the kind of detailed subsector information required in this study. I opted, therefore, for a survey of firms in the manufacturing sector.

The questionnaire for the survey, which pertains to 1978, was designed by the author along lines of a similar questionnaire for a study of Greek manufactured exports in the World Bank, with relevant modifications for the Jamaican case.[6] It was a comprehensive questionnaire, about forty pages long, requesting both qualitative and quantitative information.[7] The fieldwork was carried out during June and July 1979, and about 100 firms were contacted. Of these, seventy-one firms completed the questionnaire either totally or partially. Thus the size of the sample varies from question to question. Almost all seventy-one firms responded to the qualitative part, but only about thirty-five were able to provide the detailed information required for calculating nominal and effective protection coefficients discussed in Chapter 5. Table 1-3 summarizes the overall coverage of the sector for the seventy-one firms.

Although the response to the questionnaire was generally good, and although every effort was made to collect complete and consistent data for each firm, there are a number of biases in the structure of the sample.[8] First, almost all firms in the sample were medium- or large-scale producers by Jamaican standards, employing more than ten persons and with sales in 1978 in excess

6. Demetrious Papageorgiou, "Export Promotion Policies in Less Developed Countries: The Case of Greece" (Washington, D.C.: World Bank, 1977; processed).The questionnaire is presented in the appendix.

7. The survey was financed by the Premier Investment Corporation, a wholly owned subsidiary of the Bank of Jamaica, and received the support of the JMA. The survey was coordinated by Mr. Tapper of the consulting firm of A. B. and M. E. Associates, and ten students of the University of the West Indies and the College of Arts, Science, and Technology assisted in the fieldwork.

8. In addition to the initial four man-days allocated to each firm for completing the questionnaire, there were several follow-ups for obtaining specific missing data, removing inconsistencies, or finding the reasons for apparently odd-looking data.

Table 1-3. *Number of Large Establishments and Gross Output*
in Manufacturing, 1978

Subsector	Number of large-scale establishments			Gross value of output (J$million)		
	Total	Sample	Sample as a percentage of total	Total	Sample	Sample as a percentage of total
Food processing	157	6	4	442	75	17
Beverages	8	2	25	179	24	13
Tobacco	7	2	28	89	7	8
Textiles[a]	136	8	6	110	14	13
Footwear	29	2	7	32	1	3
Leather products	4	2	50	8	1	12
Furniture	44	5	11	61	6	10
Paper and paper products	57	4	7	98	5	5
Metal products	119	6	5	425	36	8
Chemicals	78	8	10	82	34	41
Other	114	26	23	569	57	10
Total	753	71	9	2,095	260	12

a. Includes garments.
Source: Sample data from the manufacturing survey. Data for total number of large-scale establishments and gross output are from worksheets of the Department of Statistics.

of J$500,000. No conclusions can, therefore, be drawn for small-scale enterprises, although some of the problems encountered by them are alluded to in the study. Second, the subsectors were not evenly covered by the sample. Only 3 percent of the value of output in the footwear subsector is included, whereas 41 percent in the chemicals subsector is included. The coverage is smaller for the calculations of industrial protection. Third, in some cases there is a substantial variance within the subsectors of such indicators as factor-intensity, dependence on imports, capacity utilization, and nominal and effective protection. It is important, therefore, to bear in mind that generalizations might not be appropriate for all firms or all products within a subsector. Finally, certain specific assumptions had to be made for the effective protection calculations that are described in Chapter 5. Although these assumptions are not believed to impart a significant bias to the results, the estimates should nonetheless be treated with caution and regarded as broad indicators of the overall picture of the sector.

Structure of the Study

Chapter 2 deals with the industrial incentives that have been provided to "approved" firms—firms that have been selected by the Ministry of Industry and Commerce to receive incentives—since the 1950s. These incentives are described, and the main characteristics of the incentive firms and of the costs and benefits of these incentives are discussed.

Chapter 3 describes the evolution of the sector since World War II. After a brief discussion of the early postwar developments in the sector, the chapter follows the growth of manufacturing activities between 1956 and 1976, and finally concentrates on the developments in the sector after 1976. It shows the extent to which measures such as tariffs, quantitative restrictions, and exchange rate affected the structure of the sector.

In Chapter 4 some of the effects of these government policies on the sector are enumerated and quantified. The key aspects of factor-intensity, dependence on imports, industrial concentration, and capacity utilization for Jamaica's manufacturing sector are studied, using data from the survey.

Chapter 5 deals specifically with the extent of protection provided to the manufacturing sector as a whole and to the constituent subsectors, based on sample firms. It illustrates the bias that exists against exporting in general and exporting to non-CARICOM countries in particular.[9]

Finally, Chapter 6 examines the prospects for Jamaica's manufacturing over the next few years, dealing with both macroeconomic issues relevant to the subject and assessing the comparative advantages of the main exporting subsectors.

9. The Caribbean Community (CARICOM) includes Antigua, Barbados, Belize, Dominica, Grenada, Guyana, Jamaica, Montserrat, Trinidad and Tobago, St. Kitts-Nevis-Anguilla, St. Lucia, and St. Vincent. The Bahamas, although not a member, participates in the Heads of Government Conference and in other areas of functional cooperation, and contributes to the budget of the secretariat.

Summary and Conclusions

Jamaica's varied manufacturing sector registered impressive real growth during 1950–73, averaging about 7 percent a year. Between 1974 and 1978, however, there was a decline of about 4 percent a year. What led to the impressive performance during the early period, and, equally important, what factors led to its decline in recent years? Furthermore, how did the various industrial and trade policies affect the structure of the sector?

Industrial incentives

An important factor in the initiation of industrial activity in Jamaica was the granting of industrial incentives during the 1950s in the form of income tax exemptions for specified numbers of years, duty-free imports of raw materials and machinery, generous depreciation allowances, and provisions for tax-free dividends. Detailed data on the costs and benefits of the incentive schemes and the characteristics of the firms approved under these schemes are extremely scarce. The data used in this study indicate that these incentives were an important factor in fostering industrial activity until the mid-1960s, but thereafter their importance was considerably reduced, owing to the imposition of quantitative restrictions on imports and the adoption of other trade and exchange policies. These incentives now appear excessively generous, even though their cost to the central government (in the form of revenue losses arising from corporate tax revenue forgone, individual income tax forgone on distributed dividends, and customs duties exempted) is substantially less than is generally alleged.

The results of this study indicate that the present incentive legislation should be modified. In particular, the tax-exempt period should be shorter (say, five years instead of the present nine or ten years), with the possibility of extension when necessary and advisable on the basis of performance. On the question of distribution of dividends, tax exemptions of dividends encourage investors to distribute profits of the concessionary period before its end, as any distribution thereafter would be taxed. In view of the government's objective of encouraging profit retention for reinvestment, there is a case for limiting the exemption, at least for domestic investors.

Quantitative import restrictions

Although the industrial incentives played an important role in the initiation of manufacturing sector activity in Jamaica, the continuation of the generally high rates of growth during most of the 1960s and early 1970s was largely the consequence of several other trade policies, particularly the imposition of quantitative import restrictions. The government first instituted a system of quantitative restrictions and import licensing around 1965. The extent of the gradual proliferation of these restrictions can be gauged from the fact that at the time of independence in 1962, there were only 50 items on the restricted list of imports, and by 1979 this number had increased to 334.

Quantitative restrictions are applied to products originating outside the CARICOM area on the basis of protective and balance of payments criteria. In general, the size of the quota has been determined by the gap between domestic demand and domestic supply. Thus, where an approved firm's installed capacity can meet domestic demand, it is subject to no foreign competition. In addition, it is rare for more than one firm to be approved for the same product, although nonapproved firms can in theory enter the market. Since a potential investor can usually find alternative products that would accord him approved status, there are powerful barriers to domestic competition once the initial firm has been established. Before protection is granted, the manufacturer has to satisfy the government that his ex-factory price will be no higher than the cost of equivalent imports at c.i.f. (cost, insurance, freight) prices plus the customs duty that would be levied. Not all of the products produced under protection are subject to price control, however, and prices are not checked again after protection has been granted. The size of the import quota is enlarged only in case of actual or impending shortages. The government has rarely used this measure to counter price rises, and the recent balance of payments problems have made the quotas even more restrictive. In short, quantitative restrictions and the accompanying import quotas have provided an unusually generous incentive for import-substituting firms, the benefits of which far exceed those accruing from the industrial incentives and other policy measures.

Tariffs

In the presence of quantitative restrictions, the Common External Tariff of CARICOM, which is the main fiscal instrument of protection (and is applied to non-CARICOM imports), plays a far less important protectionist role. Internal price levels are determined for most domestically produced goods by the degree of restrictiveness of the licensing system, and, as mentioned, earlier, this is exercised without reference to border prices or the equivalent ad-valorem price effect of the tariff. In the past, tariffs in Jamaica have been primarily to bring in revenue, and, except for beverages and tobacco products, the levels of tariff are not inordinately high. Since 1968, when Jamaica joined CARIFTA (The Caribbean Free Trade Association, the predecessor of CARICOM), exemptions have been conceded across the board for many inputs, thereby reducing the role of the tariff as a source of fiscal revenues, but increasing its role as a source of effective protection. The implication, therefore, is that although the reduction or removal of quantitative restrictions would reduce the bias against exporting in relation to production for the domestic market, reduction in the bias against exporting to non-CARICOM countries would additionally require some changes in the tariff structure.

Performance and structure

There are many, varied reasons for the decline of the manufacturing sector after 1973. The protection provided by the quantitative restrictions and other trade policies was heavily biased toward import-substitution and discouraged exports of manufactured goods. This may have been a feasible strategy for an economy with a larger domestic market, but in the case of Jamaica, the possibilities for further profitable import substitution were substantially exhausted by the early 1970s. On the export side, the fixed exchange rate that prevailed during 1973–76, a period of high inflation in Jamaica, clearly eroded the financial incentives to exporters. Moreover, large wage increases affected Jamaica's export competitiveness in those subsectors, such as garments, in which exports are particularly sensitive to wage increases. The problems of the sector were aggravated by acute shortages of imported raw materials after 1976 and by the emigration of a large portion of the entrepreneurial class.

How have the industrial and trade policies of the past two decades affected the structure of the manufacturing sector? The combination of duty-free, or low-duty, imports of capital goods, the choice of products accorded approved status under the incentive laws, the generous depreciation allowances, and quantitative restrictions on final products have encouraged rather capital-intensive investment. Moreover, much of the domestic industrial activity encouraged by the various policies has had low domestic value-added and has been highly dependent on imported inputs. The degree of industrial concentration in terms of the number of firms in each subsector indicates that production is monopolistic or oligopolistic. There are only three main subsectors that have low industrial concentration in both sales and employment: garments, furniture, and footwear.

Machinery and equipment in most subsectors are underutilized. The duty-free, or low-duty, imports of machinery and other macroeconomic policies, together with security problems for night work, have been some of the key reasons for excess capacity. Another specific reason for the existence of excess capacity in certain subsectors, such as pharmaceuticals, has been the restrictive nature of some of the licensing agreements of the so-called franchised firms. These firms operate under a foreign trademark to produce or distribute a product or service, but are restricted to selling in certain specific markets. Finally, over the past few years, two factors have become predominant in explaining the present low capacity utilization rates: the shortage of imported raw materials and the low level of domestic demand resulting from the government's stabilization program. Only one shift a day is the norm, with about 80 percent of the sample firms operating on this basis. A few garment, textile, and electrical appliance firms operate two shifts, and there are occasionally three shifts in food processing industries that produce perishables and in metal works, chemicals, rubber, and plastic industries, where the high costs of shutting down and starting up appear to dominate other considerations.

This study attempts to quantify the degree of protection on domestic sales, on exports to CARICOM, and on exports to other markets in order to measure the extent of discrimination against exports. The overall picture of the manufacturing sector that emerges confirms the generally held view of a highly protected domestic market, with a strong bias against exports in general and exports to non-CARICOM countries in particular. Various indicators of protection are provided in Chapter 5.

Prospects for expansion

There is evidence that the possibilities for further profitable import substitution in the small economy have been virtually exhausted. Any substantial new increases in manufacturing growth can be achieved only through a strong export drive. Adequate performance in manufactured exports will depend on several factors including, but not limited to, the following:

a. The extent to which the bias against exporting, referred to earlier, is reduced; currently the export market is viewed as a residual market after the lucrative domestic demand has been satisfied, except for items such as cigars, beverages, garments, and certain kinds of processed foods;

b. The ability of the government to adhere to realistic exchange rate and income policies;

c. The availability of imported inputs for Jamaica's import-dependent manufacturing sector;

d. The capacity of the entrepreneurs and the government to resolve, or at least to circumvent, such specific problems as shortages of skilled personnel, inadequate linkage with agriculture, problems of shipping, and so forth;

e. The ability of the government to provide adequate support through infrastructure, credit, and promotional activity through JECIC and JNEC; and

f. The ability of the government to assure the private sector, which dominates manufacturing, of its commitment to a mixed economy and of its new emphasis on export promotion.

In the short run, manufactured exports to CARICOM countries are expected to be significantly higher than those to non-CARICOM countries. The attractiveness of the CARICOM market derives in large measure from the relatively generous terms of the criteria of origin, the protection afforded by the Common External Tariff, and the fact that access to CARICOM market requires the least adjustment by Jamaican manufacturers for promotional activity, packaging, and so forth. Moreover, as a result of the depressed domestic market, some production will continue to be diverted to the CARICOM market. There is no guarantee, however, that, when the domestic market picks up and if the present asymmetry in profitability against exports persists, these exports to CARICOM would not level out or even decline. In any case, the small size of the CARICOM market precludes the possibilities of large-scale increases in exports to that market.

Looking at specific items which could be exported to the non-CARICOM markets (mainly the United States, the United Kingdom, and Canada), prospects appear bright for processed foods, liqueurs, cigars, and garments and less favorable for rum and furniture. Specific problems and prospects of these items are examined in detail in Chapter 6.

In short, prospects for Jamaica's manufactured exports crucially depend on the extent to which the bias against exporting can be reduced and on the ability of the government to continue its policies oriented toward exports. Once these conditions are fulfilled, substantial demand exists abroad for Jamaica's exports. There are constraints on the supply side, such as inadequate supplies of domestic agricultural inputs, shortages of skilled manpower, foreign exchange shortages, and poor condition of some plant and equipment, but these are surmountable. Finally, although the CARICOM market has served Jamaica well, its size is limited. Jamaica's manufactured exports can grow significantly only through expansion to non-CARICOM markets.

2

Legislation for Industrial Incentives

An important instrument used by Jamaica to initiate and direct its industrial development has been the granting of tax concessions and other fiscal incentives. The primary incentives legislation in the industrial field has been the Industrial Incentives Law (IIL) of 1956, which replaced the earlier Pioneer Industries Encouragement Law (PIEL). Some firms, however, continue to operate under the older legislation. The specific encouragement of export industries is incorporated in the Export Industries Encouragement Law (EIEL). The criteria for granting concessions and the nature of the concessions differ among the various laws.

Industrial Incentives Law (IIL)

Under this law, concessions are provided to "approved products." Two separate classes of approved products are designated: "new products" and "other" approved products. A product may be designated a new product if less than 20 percent of the national market is being supplied by existing approved manufacturers. A company manufacturing a new product is granted an income tax exemption for up to ten years, commencing within three years of the date on which the company starts production. This period may be extended up to fifteen years in designated special development areas in the country. Products other than new products may be placed on the approved products list provided the conditions of manufacture of these products fulfill various

16

criteria as regards labor intensity, utilization of Jamaican raw materials and skills, and effects on existing industries. Each application for operation under the IIL is reviewed by the Jamaica Industrial Development Corporation (JIDC), which makes recommendations to the Minister for Industry and Commerce on whether the prospective investor should be given initial approval to manufacture the approved product. Products not already on the approved list may be added to the list on the judgment of the same officials.

Certain additional concessions are granted to manufacturers of both new and other approved products. These include exemption from income tax on dividends distributed during the period of tax exemption, as well as duty-free import of materials required for factory construction, alteration, reconstruction, and extension. An approved enterprise may not, without prior permission, use the approved factory building for any other purpose than the manufacture of the approved product.

Export Industry Encouragement Law (EIEL)

This law provides concessions for industries manufacturing exclusively for export markets. The concessions provided are the same as provided for new products under the IIL, with an additional entitlement for the continuous duty-free importation of raw materials and items for repair and replacement of equipment. All production must be performed in-bond, that is, products manufactured under this law may not be sold in Jamaica except to another export manufacturer for use in the manufacture of another export product.

In December 1974 the Jamaican Parliament passed the Industrial Incentives (Regional Harmonization) Act of 1974, which attempts to harmonize policies and trade in manufactures among CARICOM countries. The scheme provides the following five benefits:

a. Exemption from income tax for a stated number of years for an approved product.
b. Relief from tonnage tax (now abolished) and customs duty

on plant and equipment, machinery, spare parts, and raw materials throughout the incentive period.

c. Carry-forward of aggregate net losses for five years after the end of a tax exemption.

d. Depreciation deduction, called an "initial allowance," not exceeding 20 percent of any capital expenditure incurred on plant equipment and machinery after the tax exemption has expired.

e. Provision for tax-free dividends.

The number of years for which benefits may be granted depends upon two criteria: whether the enterprise is approved as an enclave type and wholly export-oriented undertaking under the EIEL, in which case it may enjoy the available benefits for ten years, or whether the enterprise is approved under the IIL, in which case the precise number of years vary with the level of local value-added involved in operating the enterprise.

In the latter case, domestic value-added is estimated by deducting from ex-factory sales all direct and indirect inputs imported from non-CARICOM countries, all factor payments to non-CARICOM countries, and the legal depreciation charged to capital goods imported from non-CARICOM countries.[1] The value-added thus calculated is inflated by a local labor weight factor according to the formula:

$$V = v(1 + w),$$

where V = weighted domestic value-added, v = domestic value-added as a percentage of sales, and w = wage bill to CARICOM nationals as a percent of sales.

The value of V determines the maximum number of years for which Jamaica, according to the scheme, may grant income tax and custom duty relief to any given firm. For V of 50 percent or more, the maximum period is nine years; for V between 25 and 50 percent, the maximum period is seven years; and for V between 10 and 25 percent, it is five years. For higher capital-

---

1. This paragraph and the following one are based heavily on Demetrious Papageorgiou's "Jamaica Manufacturing Exports: Issues and Prospects" (Washington, D.C.: World Bank, March 1978; processed).

intensive projects, however, the scheme stipulates that such projects may receive up to nine years' relief from income taxes and customs duty, irrespective of the project's domestic value-added, provided that the project's capital investment is at least US$25 million. If an established firm is serving 60 percent of the domestic market, no other company within the industry may be declared an approved enterprise.

In addition to the above provisions, firms may be granted relief from income tax liability on profits from exports to countries outside CARICOM. Such concessions from income tax are available to enterprises not originally approved under EIEL or whose period of enjoyment of such benefits has expired. Under such concessions, tax credits must not exceed the income tax liability on the full amount of export profits of the approved enterprise from the manufacture of the approved product. Relief is granted on the basis of the following schedule (figures are in percentages):

Share of export profits in total profits (percent)	Maximum income tax relief of the tax chargeable (percent)
10 to 20.9	25
21 to 40.9	35
41 to 60.9	45
61 or more	50

All incentive approvals since 1974 have been governed by conditions laid down in the Regional Harmonization Act, and IIL and EIEL have been appropriately amended.

Distribution of Incentive Approvals

Detailed data relating to the costs and benefits of the incentive schemes and the characteristics of the approved firms are either unavailable or scattered among the various monitoring agencies. Moreover, revenue departments do not keep records on filed returns or on the revenue costs of the schemes.[2] The JIDC,

2. Paul Chen-Young, "A Study of Tax Incentives in Jamaica," *National Tax Journal*, vol. 20, no. 3 (September 1967), analyzes Jamaica's experience with incentives schemes for 1950–64.

Table 2-1. *Distribution of Incentive Approvals, 1950 to 1978*

Kind of approval	1950–55	1956–60	1961–65	1966–70	1971–78ᵃ	Total
IIL firms	0	16	92	95	78	281
In production	0	10	38	49	58	155
Ceased production	0	1	20	26	17	64
Never in production	0	5	34	20	3	62
EIEL firms	0	7	26	50	63	146
In production	0	3	2	10	15	30
Ceased production	0	3	20	33	42	98
Never in production	0	1	4	7	6	18
PIEL firms	15	8	9	3	0	34
In production	12	2	4	0	0	18
Ceased production	1	6	5	3	0	15
Never in production	2	0	0	0	0	2
Total for period	15	31	127	148	141	462

Note: Not included in this are the Ariguanabo Company, Ltd., which operates under the Textile Industry Encouragement Law (TIEL) and the Caribbean Cement Company, Ltd., which was approved under the Cement Industry Encouragement Law (CIEL).

a. Includes thirty-seven IIL approvals and eleven EIEL approvals after the 1974 Regional Harmonization of Industrial Incentives.

Source: JIDC.

however, is invested with the operational responsibility for these incentives schemes and has information on the number of approvals granted, the number of firms in production and ceasing production, and so forth. Until 1973 data were also collected on the employment, payroll, sales (domestic and foreign), and capital investment of the incentive firms. Table 2-1 summarizes the distribution of incentive approvals for 1964–78. A number of observations can be made about the pattern of incentive approvals.

a. Most approvals under IIL took place around the mid-1960s, whereas most approvals under EIEL occurred thereafter.
b. There was a significant slowdown of approvals under EIEL after 1969, but it picked up again after the 1974 signing of the CARICOM Harmonization Agreement.
c. A significantly higher proportion of IIL approvals than EIEL approvals actually started production.
d. A significantly lower proportion of IIL approvals than EIEL approvals closed down after beginning production.

Suggested explanations for the pattern of the distribution of incentive approvals are provided in Chapter 3 in the broader context of exchange and trade regulations that influenced the performance of the overall manufacturing sector.

Characteristics of Incentive Firms

The very way in which the industrial incentives were framed led to a dualistic structure of the manufacturing sector. Firms producing under EIEL produced exclusively for the export market, whereas firms producing under IIL (and PIEL) produced almost totally for the domestic market.[3] There are several key differences between firms operating under the two kinds of legislation.

---

3. For every year between 1965 and 1973, the ratio of export sales to total sales for firms approved under IIL (and PIEL) was, as an aggregate, less than 10 percent. Detailed annual data beyond 1973 are unavailable.

Table 2-2. Ownership Pattern of Firms Operating under Incentive Legislation, 1970 to 1973
(number of firms)

Ownership	1970		1971		1972		1973		Average percent, 1970–73	
	IIL	EIEL	IIL	EIEL	IIL	EIEL	IIL	EIEL	IIL	EIEL
100 percent foreign	23	29	21	28	20	22	22	16	14.6	64.6
United States	11	28	10	27	9	21	11	15	7.0	61.9
United Kingdom	6	0	6	0	6	0	7	0	4.3	0
Canada	5	1	5	1	4	1	3	1	2.9	2.7
Netherlands	0	0	0	0	1	0	0	0	0.3	0
Panama	1	0	0	0	0	0	0	0	0.1	0
100 percent local	73	10	75	10	71	9	75	10	50.1	26.5
Joint ventures	49	3	57	1	52	4	49	5	35.3	8.9
More than 50 percent local	23	1	31	1	26	4	23	3	17.5	6.1
Less than 50 percent local	26	2	26	0	26	0	26	2	17.8	2.8
Total	145	42	153	39	143	35	146	31	100.0	100.0

Note: End of year data. The category IIL also includes firms registered under the Pioneer Industry Encouragement Law, the Textile Industry Encouragement Law, and the Cement Industry Encouragement Law.
Source: Based on annual Industrial Activity Surveys of JIDC.

Ownership

During 1970–73 approximately 40 percent of all the companies
were either wholly owned (25 percent) or controlled (15 percent)
by foreigners. The pattern of ownership was significantly different for EIEL firms than for IIL firms (Table 2-2). Approximately
68 percent of the EIEL firms were either wholly foreign-owned
(65 percent) or controlled (3 percent). Most of the wholly foreign-owned companies were U.S. companies. By contrast, only
15 percent of IIL firms were wholly foreign-owned and another
18 percent were foreign-controlled. In addition, joint ventures
were much more prevalent among the IIL firms than among the
EIEL firms.

Goods produced

Most of the EIEL firms have been involved in the production of
garments, mostly on a subcontracting basis for the U.S. market.
There have also been firms in the fields of electronics, sports
equipment, leather products, and cigar manufacturing. Under IIL
the emphasis has been on the production of chemicals, metal
products, packaging materials, pharmaceuticals, and rubber
products.

Capital-labor ratios

As can be seen from Table 2-3, capital investment per unit of
labor is significantly higher for IIL than for EIEL firms—about
sixteen times higher for the period for which data are available
(1968–73). One explanation for this is the large number of IIL
firms in such capital-intensive industries as metal products, nonmetallic mineral manufacturers, and plastics. By contrast, most
of the industries under EIEL were labor-intensive by nature,
requiring little fixed investment. Moreover, unlike firms under
IIL, those under EIEL rented nearly 90 percent of total factory
space, mostly from the JIDC.[4]

4. Chen-Young, "A Study of Tax Incentives in Jamaica."

Table 2-3. *Capital per Unit of Labor Employed for Incentive Firms, 1968 to 1973*
(J$ per employee)

Kind of firm	1968	1969	1970	1971	1972	1973	Average, 1968–73
Overall ILL firms	6,966	10,196	10,548	11,146	10,919	10,962	10,123
Metal products	4,489	5,793	5,616	5,754	5,979	6,307	5,656
Nonmetallic minerals	3,713	19,720	19,516	20,991	27,522	33,069	20,755
Chemicals	18,831	21,396	20,435	12,567	22,961	24,753	20,157
Rubber products	n.a.	n.a.	71,762	12,567	10,812	9,234	n.a.
Plastic products	4,297	3,199	3,514	3,761	7,533	6,200	4,751
Containers and packaging	7,027	6,910	2,382	7,521	7,486	7,899	6,537
Electrical products	2,708	2,776	1,380	3,861	4,819	4,480	3,337
Food	6,041	7,518	6,849	7,953	6,996	6,950	7,051
Pharmaceuticals[a]	n.a.	n.a.	7,627	6,753	6,704	8,303	n.a.
Textiles[b]	n.a.	n.a.	11,459	5,712	6,206	6,216	n.a.
Paper products	n.a.	n.a.	874	41,896	27,552	23,873	n.a.
Miscellaneous[c]	5,876	9,142	20,768	17,737	10,973	12,007	12,750
Overall EIEL firms	525	379	580	554	773	868	613
Clothing	506	436	289	307	288	226	342
Leather products	499	126	198	192	276	460	292
Miscellaneous	591	378	1,509	1,377	1,539	1,812	1,201

Note: Capital investment in land, buildings, and machinery.

n.a. Not available.

a. Including toilet preparations.

b. Excluding clothing.

c. For 1968 and 1969, also includes rubber products, pharmaceuticals, textiles, and paper products.

Source: JIDC.

In summary, foreign ownership has been much more predominant among EIEL firms than among IIL firms. The former have been involved in the production of labor-intensive items, with a considerable amount of this production on a subcontracting basis primarily for the U.S. market. By contrast, almost all the production of IIL firms has been directed at the domestic market and with the aim of import-substitution, and production processes have been very capital-intensive, particularly in relation to those in EIEL firms.

Costs and Benefits of Incentives

As already stated, relevant data on key aspects of the incentives are extremely scarce. In the past, less attention had been given to monitoring both the activities approved and their economic effect, and relatively more emphasis had been placed on the preapproval scrutiny. The situation has not improved significantly. Any analysis of the pros and cons of the incentives is, therefore, bound to be less rigorous than might be desirable.

The earliest, and perhaps the only, analysis of the costs and benefits of the industrial incentives was carried out by Chen-Young.[5] Although the study is somewhat dated, covering Jamaica's experience with incentives between 1950 and 1964, it does shed light on some issues that may have considerable relevance today. In particular, Chen-Young has argued that the key factors affecting the investment decisions of domestic entrepreneurs were the existence of monopolistic conditions and the assurance of a guaranteed market by the protective trade policies of the government. Indeed, fewer than 5 percent of the firms interviewed by him even mentioned tax incentives as an important factor in the decision to invest. For foreign investors, particularly those based in the United States, other factors, such as an agreement for tax sparing in the home country were far more important than the incentives themselves.

In a larger sense, the incentive schemes cannot be dissociated from the various trade and exchange regulations which com-

5. Ibid.

Table 2-4. *Compensation of Employees for Incentive Firms,*
1965 to 1973
(J$ million)

Kind of firm	1965	1969	1970	1971	1972	1973
Incentive firms	n.a.	13.9	14.6	18.5	21.9	30.3
IIL firms[a]	n.a.	10.8	11.5	14.9	18.6	27.2
EIEL firms	n.a.	3.1	3.1	3.6	3.3	3.1
All manufacturing	n.a.	70.2	77.4	84.4	103.2	128.7
Incentive firms as a percentage of total manufacturing	1.3	19.8	18.9	21.9	21.2	23.5

n.a. Not available.
a. Including PIEL firms.
Source: JIDC and Department of Statistics.

plemented them and which are discussed in the next chapter. Even in the narrower sense of government revenues forgone, however, information is extremely difficult to come by.

These revenue losses would be of three sorts: corporate tax revenue forgone, individual income tax forgone on distributed dividends, and customs duties relieved. No information is available on the revenue losses owing to distribution of dividends. The last reliable figures available on corporate tax revenues forgone are for 1965. In that year, deductions permitted on account of IIL (including PIEL) and EIEL were about J$1.4 million, or about 5 percent of the total taxes collected from other companies.[6] If this proportion stayed the same, the absolute loss in 1973 (the last year for which systematic data on employment, payroll, and investment of the incentive firms are available) would have been about J$2.5 million. In fact, however, the importance of incentive firms in manufacturing appears to have increased considerably between 1965 and 1973. As is clear from Table 2-4, the payrolls of firms under IIL (including PIEL) and EIEL, as a proportion of wages and salaries paid in the manufacturing sector, grew

6. The category, "other companies," captures the corporate tax payments of all companies except the bauxite companies.

from 1.3 percent in 1965 to 23.5 percent in 1973. If this increase had been reflected in the relation of the tax liability of these incentives companies to the taxes actually paid by all companies, the figure would rise to at least J$5 million. This figure is almost certainly an underestimate, since in the 1965 base period several firms had just commenced operations, and the share of EIEL firms, which were comparatively less profitable, was greater. More recent data are available on customs duties forgone, but they are somewhat less meaningful since so many other exceptions are made to the tariff schedules as well. For what it is worth, in 1971 customs duties forgone because of IIL (including PIEL and the Textile and Cement Encouragement Laws) totaled about J$0.4 million, whereas the duties forgone because of EIEL were more substantial, J$2.7 million. The estimated figure for 1973 for custom duty exemptions for all incentive firms would be at least about J$3 million. Thus the total revenues forgone under the incentives legislation, excluding those owing to distribution of dividends, in 1973 is tentatively estimated to have been about J$8 million. In recent years, fewer firms have been granted approved status, and extensions of the exemptions have been limited. The total number of firms approved and operating declined from 246 in 1974 to 73 in 1978. On this basis, the total revenues forgone under the incentives schemes is estimated at J$6 million to J$7 million.

On the benefits side, although the government initially intended to grant approvals for products "of economic and noneconomic benefit to Jamaica and which are likely to have a beneficial effect on numbers employed and gross wages," the results have been mixed at best, thanks to the vague nature of the legal provisions, the virtual absence of supporting administrative guidelines, and the poor monitoring by responsible agencies after approval. Because of the highly capital-intensive nature of most of the operations, the effect on employment has been fairly small, except for the second half of the 1960s. Chen-Young estimated the contribution of the approved firms to value-added in manufacturing in 1963 to have been only 18 percent of the total manufacturing value-added. Similarly, Jefferson estimated that this contribution in 1968 was no more than 20 percent.[7] More recent estimates are not available. Since most of the new industries have been of the "screwdriver," variety with low value-added and limited backward linkages and with high import-intensity, the local value-added has been made in many cases at the expense of the consumer in the form of higher prices and poor quality of finished goods.[8] On the basis of data prepared by the Income Tax Department for 1977, it can be concluded that pretax rates of return on equity for a sample of incentive firms in that year have been from 40 to about 75 percent.[9]

In most developed and developing countries the sacrifice of tax revenue has been justified as a small cost necessary to induce foreign as well as domestic entrepreneurs to invest in productive activities. As already stated, no reliable recent data exist on the extent of the revenue sacrifice. It can be argued, however, that pretax annual rates of return of between 40 and 75 percent are far too high to warrant generous tax incentives, especially considering the long duration of the exemption period. Moreover, in the absence of any tax-sparing provisions in their home countries, the incentives granted to foreign investors were of limited value. This was especially true of companies based in the United States. Neither their after-tax nor cash flow positions on repatriated profits was altered. In effect, the Jamaica Treasury's loss became the U.S. Treasury's gain. Finally, the revenue loss was even less justified, since both domestic and foreign investment was only marginally influenced by tax considerations.

The general conclusion that emerges is that the exemption periods of the incentives have been unnecessarily generous, given the very high rates of return to investment of these firms. In addition, it is not clear whether it is desirable to exempt all of the profits of a foreign investor or even that this benefit does, in

---

7. See Owen Jefferson, *The Post-War Economic Development of Jamaica* (Kingston, Jamaica: University of the West Indies, 1972).

8. "Screwdriver" industries are those involving final assembling, packaging, and labeling. "Import-intensity" refers to the degree of dependence of production on imported inputs. These issues are discussed in the next two chapters.

9. The information was based on a sample of 111 companies, 99 under IIL and 12 under EIEL, and was restricted to approved firms that were in operation and paying taxes in 1977.

fact, accrue to him. On this basis, it may be argued that the tax incentives have involved an unnecessary sacrifice of Jamaican tax revenues.

Much more attention needs to be paid to these aspects of the incentive schemes in the future. With regard to the duration of the exemption, there may be a case for moving to initially shorter tax exemptions (say, five years), with scope for some extension when necessary and advisable on the basis of performance. In developing countries, investors (particularly foreign investors) are more interested in tax privileges that reduce their short-term risks rather than in privileges that depend on long-term profitability. On the question of distribution of dividends, tax exemptions of dividends encourages investors to distribute profits from the concessionary period before it ends, as any distribution thereafter would be taxed. In view of the government's objective of encouraging retentions for reinvestment, there is a case for limiting the exemption at least as it relates to domestic investors.

Such changes in the incentives schemes would clearly have to be coordinated throughout CARICOM, since Jamaica cannot make substantive modifications in the legislation unilaterally. The move to shorter tax exemptions is already, in a sense, envisaged under the CARICOM Harmonization Agreement, following the periodic audit of performance.

There is urgent need for coordination between the various government agencies (for example, Ministry of Industry and Commerce, JIDC, and Income Tax and Collector General's Departments) to ensure that the costs and benefits of these schemes are evaluated on a continuing basis. The burden of administering the incentives is significant and is expected to increase.

Finally, although the industrial incentives were important for initiating industrial activity, they were not the most significant determinants of the structure of the manufacturing sector in Jamaica. Other exchange and trade-related policies have combined with the industrial incentives to determine the nature of the sector. The next chapter deals with some of these aspects.

3

•-•··•--•·•--•-•··•-•··•-•··•-•··•-•··•-•··•-•··•-•··•-•··•-•··•-•··•-•··•-•··•-•··•-•··•

Evolution of the
Manufacturing Sector

Although industrial incentives played an important role in initiating manufacturing sector activity in Jamaica, the generally high growth rates of the sector continued during most of the 1960s and early 1970s largely because of several other policies on trade and exchange rates. The significance of these policies is analyzed in this chapter. After a brief description of the sector during the early post-War years, economic growth of the sector over the past two decades is examined in the context of policy instruments such as tariffs, exchange rate, and quantitative restrictions.

Early Developments in the Sector

Between 1938 and 1950 real value-added in the manufacturing sector increased at about 7 percent annually, from J$2.4 million to J$15.8 million, with much of the impressive growth rate reflecting the small base from which it started.[1] Although sugar milling operations dominated the sector in 1938, accounting for at least 40 percent of its total output, there were some factories producing rum, beer, cornmeal, copra, edible oils, cigars, cigarettes, matches, aerated waters, and ice.[2] The advent of World War II, with the concomitant shortage of imports, provided the

1. Alfred P. Thorne, "Size, Structure and Growth of the Economy of Jamaica," supplement to *Social and Economic Studies*, vol. 4, no. 4 (1955).
2. Ministry of Industry and Commerce (then Trade and Industry), "Review of Developments in Trade and Industry during the Period 1944–1954;" processed.

necessary impetus for producing import substitutes such as footwear, clothing, leather products, and processed fruit.

To a significant degree, the negative attitude of the British government toward Jamaica's industrialization in those early years had a debilitating effect on the economic growth of the sector. This attitude was largely based on fear that such developments would encourage manufacturing that would decrease British exports to the Jamaican market.[3] In the face of this hostile attitude, those enterprising members of the community who were not engaged in agriculture and who had access to capital were forced to enter the distributive trades, primarily the distribution of imports.[4] The distributive trades continued to grow through the mid-1970s, but then declined because of balance of payments problems, the setting up of the State Trading Corporation (monopolizing imports in many categories of goods), and the absorption of import premiums after the exchange rate adjustments.[5]

To some extent, this bias against manufacturing was removed in the 1950s, particularly after the government set up the Jamaica Industrial Development Corporation (JIDC) in 1952. The corporation was to "stimulate, facilitate, and undertake the development of industry" through financial and technical assistance to new industries, to industries that would either reduce imports or increase exports, and to industries that are labor intensive. The corporation also provided factory space at moderate rentals on its industrial sites, with access to all utilities. Its role as a provider of loan finance was later transferred to the Development Finance Corporation, later renamed Jamaica Development Bank.

Evolution of the Sector between 1956 and 1976

As mentioned earlier, one of the main factors in the initial impetus for the growth of manufacturing was the passing of

3. F. W. Pitman, "The Development of the British West Indies, 1700–1763," New Haven, 1977.

4. Owen Jefferson, *The Post-War Economic Development of Jamaica* (Kingston, Jamaica: University of the West Indies, 1972).

5. These issues are discussed later.

industrial incentives legislation. The key aspects of the two main sets of laws, the Industrial Incentives Law (IIL) and the Export Industry Encouragement Law (EIEL), both passed in 1956, led to the independent growth of firms producing almost exclusively for either the domestic or for the export markets. In view of this dualistic growth pattern, the importance of the various factors for import-substituting domestic production and those for export production are assessed.

Growth of import substitution

For several years in the mid-1960s output in the manufacturing sector rose faster than the overall GDP. Although growth in domestic agricultural processing industries tended to be rather slow, reflecting the sluggishness of farm output, the rest of the manufacturing sector expanded rapidly, by an average of 10.5 percent a year in 1962–67, compared with a 7.5 percent growth for total GDP. The industries that showed the largest increases were chemicals, cement, furniture, metal products, and a variety of other manufacturers.[6] This performance of the manufacturing sector was largely the result of a process of import substitution fostered initially by the industrial incentives. From 1961 to 1963 the rate of growth of these industries was to an important degree affected by uncertainties incident to Jamaica's transition to independence, which led the industrial community to adopt a "wait-and-see" attitude. The policies of the government in the newly independent country rapidly restored the confidence of the private sector. The growth rate of these industries, however, slowed down significantly after 1966, when opportunities for easy import substitution became less abundant. The government then instituted a rigorous system of quantitative restrictions expressly to provide additional protection to these industries.

In theory, quantitative restrictions and import licensing had existed in Jamaica long before the mid-1960s. The Trade Admin-

---

6. The fast rate of growth of the cement subsector was specifically a consequence of a construction boom during those years whereas the growth of furniture and fixtures was partially related to the growth in residential and hotel construction. See Jefferson, *The Post-War Economic development of Jamaica*.

istrator's Office was created in 1938, essentially as a war-time measure designed to allocate limited imports. The function of import restrictions changed from economic to political in the 1950s, when trade restrictions were imposed against South Africa and certain communist countries. Perhaps the only quantitative restrictions and import quotas being applied truly as a tool for protection during the 1950s were in the fledgling footwear industry, which was threatened by strong foreign competition. An import quota was established in 1952, and the industry grew rapidly thereafter under this umbrella of protection.

It was not until the mid-1960s, however, that quantitative restrictions became a deliberate policy instrument to influence the development of domestic industry. Essentially, this function of quantitative restrictions has remained the same up to the present, although recently balance of payments considerations have become much more important. The regime has become much more restrictive over time, as shown in Table 3-1. There were only about 50 items on the restricted list of imports just before independence in 1962. By 1968 this number had risen to 158, by 1973 to about 200, and by 1979 to 334. The current list consists mainly of consumer goods, but includes 26 intermediate products and raw materials and 36 in the capital goods category. In practice the number of restricted items is, of course, much greater since restricted items are sometimes defined in as broad terms as "Clothing—all types and materials." Similarly, the item, "Pharmaceutical preparations" has at least 25 items under

Table 3-1. *Number of Items under Quantitative or Absolute Import Restrictions, 1961 to 1979*

Product	1961	1964	1968	1973	1979
Consumer goods	44	58	128	164	272
Raw materials and intermediate goods	3	5	15	16	26
Capital goods	3	9	15	21	36
Total	50	72	158	201	334

Source: Calculated from various issues of Trade Administrator Department, *Proclamations, Rules, and Regulations* (Kingston, irregular publication).

the subheads of hypnotics, sedatives, tranquilizers, antihista-
mines, analgesics, antibiotics, expectorants, and so forth.

Up to 1979, the "banned" list included items that were totally
banned as well as items that were subject to restricted entry.
Under the new regulations, a clear distinction is drawn between
"those items for which the intention is to institute total prohibi-
tion—a banned list—and those in respect of which the objective
is to apply a high level of restriction—a restricted list."[7] The
banned list consists only of items whose importation is totally
prohibited, regardless of their source, the purpose for which they
are required, and whether or not Jamaican funds will be used for
the transaction. It is necessarily, therefore, a short list, and no
encouragement is given to the production of such items locally.[8]
The removal of an item from, or the addition to, this list requires
Cabinet approval. The restricted list now embraces items which,
with few exceptions, were formerly on the original banned list of
imports, together with an expanded range of other items, which
have since been deemed to warrant inclusion. This list consists of
items that, "based on economic and other development objectives are subject to high, though varying, levels of restriction."
Changes in this list do not require Cabinet approval. Licenses for
the items on this list are not generally issued, but exemptions are
considered by the Trade Administrator's Office.

Quantitative restrictions are applied to products originating
outside the CARICOM area on the basis of protective and balance
of payments criteria.[9] In general, the size of the quota has been
determined by the gap between domestic demand and domestic
supply. Thus, where an approved firm's installed capacity can
meet domestic demand, it is subject to no foreign competition.
In addition, it is rare for more than one firm to be approved for
the same product, although nonapproved firms can in theory

7. Trade Administrator Department, "Proclamations, Rules, and Regulations"
(Kingston, 1978).
8. In fact, the list consists of only four items: dogs for racing; dog racing equipment;
amusement machines called "one-arm bandits"; and "prohibited" literature, charm,
dangerous drugs, and so forth, that are banned under the Customs Act.
9. CARICOM trade is free of quantitative restrictions, but the overall import quotas
established in recent years severly affected imports from Trinidad and Tobago and
Barbados, particularly during 1977.

enter the market. Since a potential investor can usually find alternative products that would accord him approved status, there are powerful barriers to domestic competition once the initial firm has been established. Before protection is granted, the manufacturer has to satisfy the government that his ex-factory price will be no higher than the cost of equivalent imports at c.i.f. prices plus the customs duty that would be levied. Not all of the products produced under protection are subject to price control, however, and prices are not checked again after protection has been granted. The size of the import quota is only enlarged in case of actual or impending shortages. The government has rarely used this measure to counter price rises, and the recent balance of payments problems have made the quotas even more restrictive.

In short, quantitative restrictions and the accompanying import quotas have provided an unusually generous incentive for import-substituting firms, and the disadvantages of the system far exceed the benefits accruing from the industrial incentives legislation, tariff protection, and over-valuation of the exchange rate. The nature of these quantitative restrictions also has had a significant effect on the structure of the manufacturing sector in terms of output, the profitability of producing for the domestic market, prices to the consumer, industrial concentration in terms of monopoly power, and capacity utilization. These issues are discussed in Chapter 4.

Because of quantitative restrictions, the Common External Tariff of CARICOM, which is the main fiscal instrument of protection and is applied to imports from outside CARICOM, plays a far less important protectionist role. Internal price levels are determined for most domestically produced goods by the degree of restrictiveness of the licensing system, and, as mentioned earlier, this is exercised without reference to border prices or the equivalent ad valorem price effect of the tariff.[10] In the past, tariffs in

10. The earliest, and perhaps the most effective, use of the tariff to provide protection was the reduction of import duties on steel, iron, nonferrous metals, crude rubber, leather, and so forth, in 1951 to encourage the establishment of secondary industries based on these inputs. The action was based on the recommendations of an investigating committee's study, "Report of the Committee on the Revision of the Customs Tariff," Government Printer, 1950.

Jamaica have served primarily to gain revenue, and, except for
beverages and tobacco products, the levels of tariff are rather
moderate, as can be seen from Tables 3-2 and 3-3. If the average
nominal tariffs for manufactured products is weighted by the
share of each sector in total manufacturing output in Jamaica in
1973, instead of by the share of imports in the CARICOM market
(as in Table 3-3), the results are different, but still show relatively
moderate levels, as is shown in Table 3-4.

The role of the tariff as a source of fiscal revenues has been
significantly reduced. In addition to the exemptions from customs duties accorded under the industrial incentive laws, since
1968 (when Jamaica joined CARIFTA) exemptions have been conceded across the board, through customs, excise, stamp duty,
and retail sales tax acts. At present, any firm can import its inputs
totally exempt of tariff duties or any other tax.[11] The 10-percent
stamp duty on all imports of raw materials, intermediate, and
capital goods (imposed purely to reduce the overall fiscal deficit
of the government in the 1978–79 budget) was removed for all
raw materials and intermediate goods after strong pressure from
manufacturers that the duty severely affected the competitiveness of Jamaican exports in the CARICOM market.[12]

In addition to customs duties and stamp duty, tariffs also
include consumption duty and the retail sales tax on excise. One
of the prime objectives of the consumption duty is to replace
revenue lost from the customs duties on sales in the CARICOM
market. The retail sales tax is a straightforward revenue tax
applying to few commodities (air conditioners, stoves, televi-
sions, record players, and refrigerators) at 10 percent and to
motor cars at 25 percent. Although an analysis of the tax structure of Jamaica is beyond the scope of this study, there is some
cascading effect of consumption duty on top of excise (and later
of the retail sales tax on excise). Such cascade makes the effective
rate of tax different from that intended by the authorities and is

---

11. Except those engaged in the manufacture of tobacco products, alcoholic beverages, soft drinks, and a few other commodities not subject to internal taxes.

12. Under the CARICOM Harmonization Agreement such a duty cannot be rebated
when goods are exported to the regional market.

Table 3-2. *CARICOM Common External Tariff*
(percent)

SITC classification	Product	Weighted average tariff[a]
0	Food	9
1	Beverages and tobacco	115
2	Crude materials	9
3	Mineral fuels	8
4	Animal and vegetable oils	15
5	Chemicals	20
6	Manufactured goods	27
7	Machinery	20
8	Miscellaneous manufactures	34
0–8	Total/average	22

a. Based on weighted averages of duty payable as a percentage of total CARICOM imports for each category.

Source: Adapted from World Bank, "Caribbean Regional Study," vol. 6 (a restricted-circulation document) (1975).

inefficient. The government realized this and took steps in the direction of a general sales tax in its 1979–80 budget.

The nominal exchange rate was not a significant instrument in terms of determining the level of domestic protection in manufacturing or altering this level for 1960 to about 1973. Throughout most of this period, Jamaica had a fixed exchange rate, except for two small adjustments in 1967 and 1973. In 1967 the Jamaican currency was devalued in U.S. dollar terms, in line with the devaluation of the pound sterling, to which it was traditionally linked. In early 1973 the link with the pound sterling was cut, and the Jamaica dollar thereafter was pegged to the U.S. dollar. The new par value implied a devaluation in 1973 of about 13 percent. At the same time domestic price increases during 1960–72 were low relative to the 1970s and in relation to its main trading partners. After 1973, however, the inflation rate in Jamaica increased rapidly compared with its main trading partners, fueled mainly by the oil price increases and large wage demands. Table 3-5 provides the changes in the nominal and real exchange rates for 1965–78.

Table 3-3. *Tariff Rates for Certain Products, 1954 to 1979*
(percent ad valorem)

Product	1954		1964		1970		1974		1976	1979
	Prefer-ential	*Gen-eral*	*Prefer-ential*	*Gen-eral*	*Prefer-ential*	*Gen-eral*	*Prefer-ential*	*Gen-eral*		
Canned meat	10	25	10	25	12.5	30.5	12.5	27.5	15	15
Canned fish	5	15	5	15	5	15	5	15	3	3
Cereals	10	15	10	15	10	15	11.5	16.5	15	15
Raw cotton	10	15	10	15	10	15	11.5	16.5	5	5
Synthetic fibers	10	15	10	15	10	15	11.5	16.5	5	5
Petroleum	9	12	9	12	9	12	10	13	5	5
Vitamins	20	30	20	30	24.5	36.5	25	35	5	5
Perfumed oil and toilet waters	15	20	15	20	15	20	55	60	50	50
Soaps	20	30	20	30	20	30	25	35	30	30
Synthetic plastic materials	10	15	10	15	10	15	11.5	16.5	15	15
Chemical materials	10	15	10	15	10	15	11.5	16.5	30	30
Leather	10	15	10	15	10	15	11.5	16.5	15	15
Manufactures of leather	15	25	15	25	15	25	23	33	45	45
Rubber tires[a]	20	40	20	40	20	40	22	42	30	30
Plywood	10	20	10	20	10	20	12	22	20	20

Boxes and crates	0	10	0	10	0	10	0	10	0	10	30	30
Paper and paperboard	15	20	15	20	15	20	17	22	17	22	20	20
Cotton yarn and thread	20	30	20	30	20	30	23	33	23	33	15	15
Cotton fabrics[b]	10	20	10	20	10	20	11.5	22.5	11.5	22.5	40	40
Carpets	20	30	20	30	20	30	25	35	25	35	45	45
Glass[c]	9	12	9	12	9	12	10	13	10	13	0	0
Bottles	15	20	15	20	15	20	17	22	17	22	30	30
Jewelry of gold and silver	20	30	20	30	24.5	36.5	75	85	75	85	60	60
Cutlery	20	30	20	30	20	30	23	33	23	33	25	25
Machine tools[d]	0	5	0	5	0	3.5	0	3.5	0	3.5	10	10
Woodwork machinery	0	5	0	5	0	3.5	0	3.5	0	3.5	5	5
Motor vehicles	20	40	20	40	20	40	42	62	42	62	45	45
Wood furniture	30	25	30	35	36.5	42.5	37.5	42.5	37.5	42.5	45	45
Handbags (textile)	15	20	15	20	15	20	17	22	17	22	40	40
Footwear	15	27[e]	18	30	18	30	18.5	33[e]	18.5	33[e]	25	25

Note: The preferential rate, applicable to British Commonwealth countries, was abolished in 1976.

a. Excluding aircraft and tractor tires.

b. Unbleached.

c. Including broken and powdered.

d. For drilling, boring, grinding, and so forth.

e. Adjusted for specific duty.

Source: Various issues of "Customs Tariff of Import Duties and Exemptions from Duty."

To summarize, the main factor encouraging domestic import substitution in Jamaica has been the existence of quantitative restrictions and the accompanying import quotas. The industrial incentives played an important role in the setting up of the base

Table 3-4. *Average Nominal Tariffs for Manufactures*
(percent)

Industry	Weighted average tariff[a]
Food, beverages, and tobacco	32
Textiles, footwear, and leather	42
Heavy industries	22
Miscellaneous	27

a. Weights reflect share of subsector in total manufacturing output in 1973.
Source: Adapted from Inter-American Development Bank, "Pilot Study on National Accounting Parameters," Jamaica Country Report (Washington, D.C., IDB, 1977).

Table 3-5. *Nominal and Real Exchange Rates, 1965 to 1978*

Year	Official rate (J$ per US$)	Real rate (J$ per US$)	Relative price index[a] (1975 = 100)
1965	0.714	0.962	134.7
1968	0.833	1.089	130.8
1970	0.833	1.005	120.7
1971	0.767	0.914	119.2
1972	0.767	0.913	119.1
1973	0.909	1.022	112.4
1974	0.909	0.976	107.4
1975	0.909	0.909	100.0
1976	0.909	0.867	95.4
1977	1.156[b]	1.051	90.9
1978	1.532[b]	1.112	72.6

Note: Annual average rates.
a. The ratio of U.S. price index to Jamaican price index. For the United States, the wholesale price index has been used. In the absence of any such index for Jamaica, the consumer price index has been used.
b. From April 1977 to May 1978 the averages include only the special rate applicable to almost all manufacturing, rather than the less depreciated basic rate applicable to some items of import and export.
Source: Based on data from Bank of Jamaica and International Financial Statistics, IMF.

for manufacturing, but their significance was greatly eroded over time because of blanket exemptions from import duties on imports of raw materials and intermediate goods. Tariffs have been more a source of revenue rather than a source of protection. Changes in nominal and real exchange rates during the 1960s and early 1970s were insignificant, and only after 1973 did currency overvaluation become a factor enhancing the profitability of producing for the domestic rather than for the export market.

Growth of exports

In theory, import substitution and export promotion were given equal importance by the government.[13] In practice, however, the quantitative restrictions and other related policies made producing for the domestic market much more profitable than exporting, and a strong bias against exports developed. As mentioned above, the initial impetus for exporting came from the EIEL, and the value of exports after 1956 (when EIEL became applicable) increased at a substantially greater rate than before. The fastest growing subsector was clothing, where the export value increased from about J$0.2 million in 1957 to J$6.7 million in 1968. Other items have included cigars, leatherware, electronics, computer cards, and so forth.[14]

After 1969 there was a discernible decline in the growth rate of the firms receiving export incentives. In 1969 there were thirty-nine firms producing under EIEL, employing 6,367 workers and with export sales of about J$16.5 million. By 1973 the number of firms approved and in operation had declined to thirty-one,

13. The theoretical emphasis on the promotion of manufactured goods for export was so important that the government stated that it would not hinder firms producing for the export market, but using capital intensive methods, even though this would imply a conflict with the objective of job creation. See National Planning Agency, *A National Plan for Jamaica, 1957–67* (Kingston: NPA, 1957).
14. In the case of cigars, expansion of exports was not achieved without problems. In the late 1950s and early 1960s, Jamaican cigars had earned a bad reputation for uneven quality, particularly compared with the Havana cigar. Even after the United States banned the importation of Cuban cigars in 1960, imports of the Jamaican product failed to expand appreciably because cigars were being imported into the United States from other areas, such as Canary Islands. See Jefferson, *The Post-War Economic Development of Jamaica*.

employing 4,422 workers with export sales of about J$11.5 million. Put another way, of the thirty-nine firms operating under EIEL in 1969, twenty-four (or over 60 percent) ceased operation by 1973, most of them doing so well before the expiration date of their incentive.[15] Of these twenty-four firms, fourteen were clothing firms (producing mainly brassieres), three were leather goods producers, four electronics firms, and three that produced miscellaneous goods.

The explanation of this phenomenon lies mainly in the nature of the EIEL firms. These firms were, as already mentioned, firms producing entirely for export, with relatively low capital investment per employee (generally renting their factory space from the JIDC), mostly foreign-owned, and almost exclusively serving the U.S. and Canadian markets. Their activities were essentially based on low wage rates in activities such as garments, electronics, and leather goods, which traditionally attract "footloose" firms. Evidence suggests that during most of the 1960s Jamaica had a comparative advantage in such activities compared with, say, Puerto Rico.[16] Over time, however, the deteriorating political and economic situation discouraged the foreign firms from extending their approved status once it had expired.

The government that came to power in 1972 was generally perceived by the private sector as hostile to it, and this started a large flow of private capital and skilled manpower out of the country. The imposition of the bauxite levy on foreign companies in 1974, threats of unionization, and higher wage demands further aggravated the problem.[17]

In addition, Jamaica's joining of CARIFTA in 1968 and the resulting extension of the lucrative domestic market to the regional level caused the relative importance of EIEL firms in total manufacturing exports to decline. Exports of manufactured

15. Sixteen new firms started operating under EIEL between 1969 and 1973.
16. Paul Chen-Young, "A Study of Tax Incentives in Jamaica," *National Tax Journal*, vol. 20, no. 3 (September 1967).
17. Extensions of the approved status were not discouraged by the government, particularly in view of the employment consideration. Indeed, there were cases of firms who changed their names and obtained an additional ten years of exemptions.

goods from Jamaica to the CARIFTA market increased by about 50 percent (from US$5.8 million to US$8.7 million) in the first year of operation. The effect on Jamaica's exports of CARIFTA and of the faltering in performance of EIEL firms can be gauged from the fact that the percentage share in total manufacturing exports of the EIEL firms declined steadily from 52 percent in 1968, to 44 percent in 1970, to 36 percent in 1972, and to 27 percent in 1973.

As already mentioned, the fixed exchange rate that prevailed in relation to the U.S. dollar during 1973–76 in the presence of high inflation in Jamaica clearly also eroded the financial incentives to exporters, particularly those exporting to countries outside CARICOM. Finally, the latter group were also affected by the enactment of a minimum wage in 1976, which affected the garments industry in particular.

These disincentives to exporting notwithstanding, the government did take certain concrete measures during the early and mid-1970s to encourage production for foreign markets. In 1971 the Bank of Jamaica, through its subsidiary, the Jamaica Export Credit Insurance Corporation (JECIC), started a special export facility for nontraditional products in the form of insurance covering up to 80 percent of political and commercial risks of nonpayment. This was for short-term transactions up to a maximum of 180 days for consumer goods, but in special cases, it could also cover longer-term transactions. Later, during 1974 and 1975, rediscounting facilities were introduced to provide additional funds for post-shipment financing through the commercial banking system at preferential rates of 6 percent, for up to 80 percent of the value of the transaction for a maximum of 180 days. These facilities have generally worked well, providing credit facilities for Jamaican exporters similar to those provided to their main foreign competitors. In 1976, a pre-shipment rediscounting facility was introduced to provide financing for up to 60 percent of the f.o.b. export value of the goods, covering the complete import-export cycle in a manner that would increase the credit facilities of the exporter above his usual credit lines with the commercial banks and at a preferential rate of 10.5 percent as opposed to an average commercial rate of about 15 percent. The Bank of Jamaica has provided a fund of about J$30 million a year for these facilities. The pre-shipment facility had some operative problems and was not being used fully. This was mainly because the commercial banks, who were bearing the full credit risk, were not willing to expand their lines of credit to their customers, since most of them were considered to have reached the limit of borrowing.

The main benefits of the export credit system, apart from providing post-shipment credit at conditions that are similar to those of most of Jamaica's competitors, have been the subsidy element of the pre-shipment interest rate and a greater accessibility to credit when banks have been acting with great restraint despite their excess liquidity. The average financial value of this preferential interest rate, however, is of the order of no more than 0.7 percent of the f.o.b. unit value of the products exported, and not all exporters of nontraditional products have made use of it. Moreover, since 1976 exporters have been forced to use financing in external currency supplied by several foreign credit lines secured by the Bank of Jamaica, which result in effective rates considerably above the current internal commercial rate. This is due to the critical scarcity of foreign exchange that the country has been going through.

On the institutional side, the establishment of the Jamaica National Export Corporation (JNEC) in the early 1970s has been a useful benefit, particularly on the marketing side. In view of its recent growing importance, some of its primary functions are described below.

To summarize, the initial impetus provided to nontraditional manufacturing exporters under EIEL was considerably weakened during the late 1960s and early 1970s primarily because of the deteriorating political and economic situation, high wage increases, and the overvalued currency. Simultaneously, the formation of CARIFTA in 1967 (and its conversion to CARICOM) gave the Jamaican exporters a protected market. As a consequence, during 1969–76 exports to the CARICOM market increased considerably, but exports to countries outside CARICOM did not increase at all. On the whole, incentives to exporters have been significantly below those to import-substituting firms.

Developments in the Sector since 1976

Developments in the manufacturing sector after 1976 were predominantly influenced by macroeconomic factors, particularly the severe balance of payments and fiscal problems. Several problems were of particular concern to all manufacturers.

Factors hindering growth

Undoubtedly the most important limiting factor to growth of the sector was the severe shortage of imported raw materials and spare parts.[18] Particularly during 1977, when import restrictions were most severe, real value-added for the sector as a whole declined about 10 percent, with substantially larger declines in the subsectors most dependent on imports, such as paper products, petroleum refining, chemicals, and metal products (Table 3–6).

Several other developments hindered the growth of the sector. The deteriorating investment climate, particularly during 1977 and 1978, and the build-up of commercial arrears due to the overall balance of payments situation made it increasingly difficult for manufacturers to secure suppliers' credits. Debt-equity ratios were high in most cases, and commercial banks were requiring—even for larger enterprises—collaterals equivalent to two or three times the amount of the loan. There were also problems relating to the arrears situation of the Jamaica Development Bank—the main source for medium- and long-term financing—which led to a lapse in lending through most of 1977–79. The increase in the number of labor disputes and the increased burden of taxation all aggravated the situation. To some extent the situation was also clouded by the establishment of the State Trading Corporation (STC) in November 1977. Through a network of subsidiaries, it was to be responsible for importing a wide range of essential items. The emphasis

18. Evidence on this is provided in Chapter 4.

Table 3-6. *Real Growth Rates for Manufacturing Subsectors, 1975 to 1978*
(percent change)

Subsector	1975	1976	1977	1978
Food (excluding sugar)	6.9	−1.0	−11.4	−7.2
Sugar, rum, and molasses	−2.8	−0.8	−17.2	−2.6
Alcoholic beverages	6.4	−10.1	−2.3	3.9
Nonalcoholic beverages	−7.5	−3.9	8.3	−8.9
Tobacco and tobacco products	5.2	−4.1	0.2	−3.6
Textiles and wearing apparel	2.9	−8.8	−10.8	−9.1
Leather and leather products	−16.0	14.3	5.2	28.3
Footwear	16.4	−10.6	9.9	−16.2
Wood and wood products	42.1	−6.9	26.4	−35.6
Furniture	−30.3	1.7	−3.4	−25.1
Paper and paper products	1.4	−15.9	−17.4	0.0
Petroleum refining	−5.2	−14.5	−15.0	−7.7
Chemicals, rubber, and plastics	1.6	4.6	−13.2	2.7
Nonmetallic products	−1.2	−15.1	−4.9	−8.0
Machinery and metal products	5.2	−1.2	−23.5	−4.2
Other manufacturing	0.0	−3.9	−17.0	3.5
Average	2.4	−5.1	−9.6	−4.8

Note: At constant 1974 prices.
Source: Department of Statistics.

appeared to be on the Corporation's acting as bulk buyer to obtain better prices, improved facilities abroad, and lower shipping charges. Although some small manufacturers in the footwear, woodwork, and garments subsectors welcomed the STC because it considerably reduced the bias against small producers, most larger firms, at least initially, opposed the move.[19]

Effect of policy changes on exports

One important aspect of the developments since the end of 1976 has been the reduction of bias against exporting. The ex-

19. The bias resulted from the fact that although most large manufacturers import directly, small-scale enterprises are constrained to obtain their imported inputs from distributors. The price to small producers is, therefore, typically higher because it includes not only the duty paid by the distributors (which is not paid by direct-user manufacturers) but also the distributors' mark-up.

change rate adjustments since April 1977 and the depressed state of the domestic market due to the government's macroeconomic policies increased the incentive to divert sales to foreign markets.[20] In addition, the government took a series of specific measures to significantly promote exports. One of the key measures was the Certified Exporter Scheme, which gave highest priority in import licenses to exporters and linkage industries, whose outputs are used as inputs by the exporters. This priority was linked to the use of rediscounting facilities of the Export Development Fund, a pre-shipment financing facility set up with a US$30 million loan from the World Bank in 1979. To obtain such status, the producer must have exported at least US$200,000 in 1978, or 20 percent of his sales, or he must have been able to execute an export program in 1979 fulfilling such requirements. More than 100 firms were approved as certified exporters.

This group of exporters also became the target group for concentrating the scarce institutional support facilities of the public sector, expediting all kinds of bureaucratic processes and giving priority use of public services provided by state enterprises, such as air transport and port facilities. The institutional support included provision of information, training, advisory services, and deployment of consultants for international marketing and production management. The main agencies involved in executing the program were the JECIC (provision of credit), the JNEC (marketing and management), and the JIDC (production and plant design problems). The JNEC was restructured to enable it to carry out the new program of export promotion and development and to advise the government on such matters. It did this in concert with its subsidiaries, the Jamaica Export Trading Company and the Jamaica Marketing Company. JNEC increased its direct trading and promotional opera-

---

20. In mid-1979, the Jamaican dollar was worth US$0.56, compared with US$1.10 in early April 1977. The removal of many subsidies, the adjustment in prices of large public utilities (to reduce the overall fiscal gap), and the effect of devaluation on the prices of imported items implied that inflation rate (on end-of-year basis) during 1978 was 49 percent, at a time when the government was generally restricting nominal wage increases to 15 percent.

tions and gave grants to exporters for training and operational travel.

The macroeconomic policies of exchange rate adjustment and strict wage guidelines, together with some specific measures aimed at export promotion, clearly benefited the export sector by reducing some of the bias against exporting. This, together with the depressed domestic market, prompted some firms to enter the field of exporting for the first time.

If, however, devaluation and the package of measures accompanying it are to result in a sustained reduction of bias and a consequent improvement in the balance of payments, foreign exchange receipts must start to grow at a rate not significantly below the rate of growth of demand for imports. In the case of Jamaica, the time that has elapsed since the first exchange rate action of April 1977 has been too short for any significant reallocation of resources to exporting. Discussions with manufacturers revealed that quick increases in nontraditional exports might not occur for five reasons.

a. Although the manufacturers had accepted the government's declarations about the new phase of export promotion, they were waiting to see whether the new incentives continued.

b. Discussions with Jamaican exporters revealed that, in several cases, the availability of excess capacity itself did not imply that that capacity could be used to produce for foreign (especially outside CARICOM) markets because of the quality considerations of the final products. The general impression, however, was that these considerations were mainly relevant to U.S., Canadian, and British markets in view of the stricter quality requirements of those markets. It was not a significant factor for CARICOM.[21]

c. It takes time to decide to create new capacity.

d. Further lags would occur as plant and equipment were ordered and installed.

---

21. In 1978 about 55 percent of Jamaica's nontraditional manufactured exports went to CARICOM.

e. Additional time might be needed for developing foreign markets.

The short-run, therefore, is the period during which resources might begin to shift, but it does not extend to the period when export earnings would start to grow out of the capacity created in response to the altered bias of the trade regime. Clearly such a period would be a difficult one; if export earnings did not increase, it would not be easy to sustain the import liberalization necessary for export growth, and it is likely that skepticism about prospects for its success would develop.[22] This is the period during which many of the costs—including whatever price level increases and reduction in the rate of growth that may result from devaluation—are incurred, but the longer-term benefits that could result are not yet realized.

In Jamaica the transition has been somewhat less traumatic due to several factors. Perhaps the most important factor has been the large inflow of external bilateral and multilateral aid in support of the government's program agreed to with the IMF.[23] Apart from inflows from the IMF under the Extended Fund Facility and other facilities, there was a substantial increase in capital inflows that could be disbursed quickly and that were not tied to a particular project from several bilateral and multilateral sources under the Caribbean Group.[24] Gross external capital inflows (including loans related to projects), together with IMF disbursements, accounted for at least 13 percent of GDP during 1978 and 1979.

There were also other factors. In the tourist industry the responses to market and other changes are typically relatively quick and without long gestation periods. This sector registered

22. Diaz-Alejandro believes, therefore, that export promotion should precede import liberalization. See Carlos Diaz-Alejandro, "Trade Policies and Economic Development," *International Trade and Finance,* ed. Peter B. Kenen (Cambridge: Cambridge University Press, 1975).

23. The IMF program was suspended in early 1980, but negotiations were reinitiated by the new government in October 1980.

24. The Caribbean Group for Economic Cooperation in Development was formed in late 1977, under the chairmanship of the World Bank, to provide concessionary and quickly disbursing program-type assistance to the Caribbean countries. Jamaica received approximately US$55 million in both 1978 and 1979 under the arrangement.

a significant increase in foreign exchange receipts during 1978 and 1979, helped by the existing excess capacity. The relatively high world demand for Jamaica's bauxite and good weather conditions during 1977 and 1978 also helped in easing the transition.

As already mentioned, the period under consideration is too short to draw any definitive conclusions about the effect of the new economic program on the manufacturing sector's exports.[25] Some preliminary conclusions, however, may be drawn from the data for 1976–78.

To begin with, the combined effect of the flexible exchange rate and the restrictive wage policy, underlying the program agreed to with the IMF, was to reduce significantly (in U.S. dollar terms) the nominal wage rates in almost all subsectors of manufacturing. The overall wage rates of employees in large establishments declined roughly 20 percent between 1976 and 1978 (Table 3-7).[26] This development should have assisted Jamaica's prospects for manufactured exports, particularly outside CARICOM, provided the government continued to adhere to its economic program.

Table 3-8 summarizes the growth of manufactured exports to both CARICOM and the rest of the world. Whereas about two-thirds of the value of exports to countries outside CARICOM is accounted for by beverages, tobacco, and clothing (rum, liqueurs, and cigars alone account for over 55 percent), exports to the CARICOM area are more evenly distributed among the categories, the more important ones being processed foods, chemicals, perfumery and soaps, metal manufactures, electrical machinery, and miscellaneous manufactures.

As can be seen from Table 3-8, manufactured exports registered a decline, in current U.S. dollar terms, of about 8.5 percent during 1977 (a 7.1 percent decline for the CARICOM

25. The analysis is restricted to the effect of the economic program on manufacturing, rather than on the whole economy.

26. Data in Table 3-7 refer to establishments employing more than ten persons. These establishments account for about half the employment in the sector. The inclusion of small enterprises (for which data are not available) would not alter the conclusions significantly.

Table 3-7. *Index of Average Weekly Wages in Large Establishments, by Manufacturing Subsectors, 1977 and 1978*
(1976 = 100)

Subsector	1977	1978
Sugar, rum, and molasses	82.1	76.6
Bakeries	77.5	64.2
Other food manufactures	95.6	77.8
Beverages	85.5	88.0
Tobacco	71.9	69.6
Footwear	101.8	82.6
Wearing apparel	103.2	77.4
Other textile industries	88.2	88.2
Wood and wood products	92.9	82.3
Paper and paper products	92.9	76.5
Chemicals	96.8	78.8
Nonmetallic minerals	76.9	85.2
Basic metals and products	89.6	85.8
Other manufacturing	100.6	106.1
Average[a]	89.9	79.5

Note: In US$ terms. The exchange rates used were US$1.00 equals J$0.909 in 1976, J$1.156 in 1977, and J$1.532 in 1978.

a. Weighted average, the weights being the number of persons employed in each subsector.

Source: Adapted from Department of Statistics, *Employment, Earnings, and Hours in Large Establishments* (Kingston, annual issues).

region and a 9.9 percent decline for the rest) and an increase of 7.2 percent during 1978 (a 16.1 percent increase for the CARICOM region and a decline of about 2 percent for the rest). Several questions arise from an examination of the table.

a. Why was growth generally better for the CARICOM area than for the rest?

b. Why was the growth of manufactured exports generally unsatisfactory for these years?

c. Did manufacturers reduce their export prices (in US$ dollars) in response to the devaluation?

The first question was already answered earlier when it was suggested that the CARICOM market is, in a sense, an extension of the domestic market. The protection granted to exporters of

Table 3-8. *Summary of Manufactured Exports to CARICOM and Non-CARICOM Countries, 1976 to 1978*

	1976		1977		1978	
Subsector group	CARICOM	Non-CARICOM	CARICOM	Non-CARICOM	CARICOM	Non-CARICOM
	J$ million					
Manufacturing I	2.7	22.4	2.8	25.5	4.0	32.1
Manufacturing II	5.6	3.8	5.9	3.2	9.8	7.4
Manufacturing III	10.9	4.7	13.0	5.8	17.9	6.5
Manufacturing IV	3.7	1.1	5.0	1.6	8.1	2.3
Manufacturing V	10.4	1.2	12.8	1.8	20.8	1.1
Total	33.3	33.2	39.5	37.9	60.6	69.4
	US$ million					
Manufacturing I	3.0	24.6	2.4	22.1	2.6	21.0
Manufacturing II	6.2	4.2	5.1	2.8	6.4	4.8
Manufacturing III	12.0	5.2	11.2	5.0	11.7	4.2
Manufacturing IV	4.1	1.2	4.3	1.4	5.3	1.5
Manufacturing V	11.4	1.3	11.1	1.6	13.6	0.7
Total	36.7	36.5	34.1	32.9	39.6	32.2

Note: Excludes sugar and molasses; other fresh, frozen, and semiprocessed products; petroleum and petroleum products; and re-exports. The subsectors are grouped according to the share of CARICOM in total exports for each subsector (average 1976–78). Thus, Manufacturing I includes subsectors with share of CARICOM less than 25 percent (beverages, tobacco, and clothing); Manufacturing II, between 25–65 percent (leather, rubber and wood, food, and textiles); Manufacturing III, 65–75 percent (plastics, chemicals, perfumery and soaps, and miscellaneous); Manufacturing IV, 75–85 percent (pharmaceuticals, mechanical and transport equipment, nonmetallic minerals, and furniture); and Manufacturing V, more than 85 percent (metal mechanics, paper products, apparel and shoes, and electrical equipment).

Source: Department of Statistics, *"External Trade"* (Kingston, annual issues).

Table 3-9. *Excess of f.o.b. Export Prices to* CARICOM
*over f.o.b. Export Prices to Rest of the World
for Selected Products, 1976 to 1978*
(percent)

Product	1976	1977	1978	Average, 1976–78
Sweetened biscuits	137	69	35	80
Tonic food	−20	−15	35	0
Grapefruit juice (concentrated)	−25	77	7	20
Bottled rum[a]	9	21	−7	8
Rum in bulk[b]	49	65	51	55
Cordials and liqueurs	−3	−28	−16	−16
Cigars	9	0	21	10
Bottles for beer and wine	157	6	5	56
Brassieres	7	20	13	13
Average[c]	11	21	14	15

Note: Negative value signifies that CARICOM price is lower.
a. Not exceeding 80 percent proof.
b. Exceeding 80 percent proof.
c. Trade-weighted average.
Source: Adapted from Department of Statistics, *External Trade*.

member countries has made selling in this Caribbean market
much easier and profitable than, say, in the United States, Canada, or Britain. Table 3-9 shows that, for 1976–78, f.o.b. export
prices to CARICOM for certain selected items were an average of
about 15 percent above those for countries outside CARICOM. For
certain items such as sweetened biscuits, rum in bulk, and bottles
for beer and wine, the CARICOM prices were over 50 percent
higher than outside CARICOM, although prices for cordials and
liqueurs have generally been lower. In short, because of the
protected nature of the CARICOM and the fact that the economy
of the main importer of Jamaica's manufactured goods, petro-
leum-rich Trinidad and Tobago, was booming, Jamaica's exports to the region have generally done well.
    With regard to the second question, the key bottleneck has
been the tight foreign exchange situation, which resulted in
severe restrictions on the imports of raw materials and intermediate goods, particularly during 1977. Moreover, the

Table 3-10. *Index of Prices for Selected Nontraditional Exports*
to Non-CARICOM Markets, 1977 and 1978
(1976 = 100)

Product	Weight	1977	1978
Biscuits, unsweetened	0.005	97.6	82.4
Biscuits, sweetened	0.003	112.6	164.6
Tonic food	0.008	87.9	105.0
Grapefruit juice (concentrated)	0.016	75.7	114.9
Bottled rum[a]	0.018	95.1	120.0
Rum in bulk[b]	0.203	82.5	91.2
Cordials and liqueurs	0.369	97.0	85.4
Cigars	0.276	94.7	81.6
Pimento oil	0.033	89.7	99.9
Bottles for beer and wine	0.001	175.0	150.0
Brassieres	0.059	89.0	150.0
Footwear	0.008	100.8	118.0
Total/average	1.000	92.3	91.5

Note: In US$ terms.
a. Not exceeding 80 percent proof.
b. Exceeding 80 percent proof.
Source: Adapted from Department of Statistics, *External Trade*.

generally high dependence of the sector on imports has meant
that exporters have not benefited significantly from the devaluation, except those subsectors that had high local value-added.[27]
Lack of skilled manpower, which has become critical owing to
the heavy emigration of the past few years, and other supply-
related problems have exacerbated the situation. Thus, although
Jamaican manufactured exports have become more competitive,
the supply response has not been significant so far.

  With regard to the final question, there is evidence—from
both data on individual firms and aggregate data—to suggest
that Jamaican manufacturers sold some important commodities
to countries outside CARICOM at lower f.o.b. prices in 1978 than
in 1976 in terms of U.S. dollars. In the case of foreign-owned
firms, the local company generally sold the goods at lower U.S.
dollar prices to the parent company, which then passed on part of

27. This and other characteristics of the sector are discussed in the next chapter.

the lower prices to foreign consumers and used part of the new profits for more advertising and promotion. Discussions with some locally owned firms suggested that the exporters gave discounts to foreign buyers, which had the effect of reducing the per unit f.o.b. value of their goods. This evidence from individual firms is corroborated by aggregate data in Table 3-10. The data in the table are based on per unit f.o.b. values of selected items of export, and may, therefore, reflect some changes in the product mix or under-invoicing of exports. Even for items like rum in bulk (exceeding 80 percent proof), however, where product mix and under-invoicing do not appear to be a problem, the product was sold at an average f.o.b. price of US$2.74 per gallon in 1976 and US$2.50 per gallon in 1978. By contrast, the f.o.b. prices in 1978 in CARICOM were an average of about 20 percent higher than in 1976, despite declines in the prices of some items carrying a small weight (Table 3-11). A tentative conclusion is that even in the case of a very small economy such as Jamaica's,

Table 3-11. *Index of Prices for Selected Nontraditional Exports to* CARICOM *Markets, 1977 and 1978*
(1976 = 100)

Product	Weight	1977	1978
Sweetened biscuits	0.015	80.3	93.1
Tonic food	0.217	95.8	101.6
Grapefruit juice (concentrated)	0.018	180.0	165.4
Bottled rum\a	0.011	105.4	101.7
Rum in bulk\b	0.003	91.4	92.2
Cordials and liqueurs	0.009	72.1	73.7
Cigars	0.008	102.9	108.6
Medicaments	0.245	123.5	154.1
Bottles for beer and wine	0.041	75.0	65.0
Sheets of iron and steel	0.352	96.8	108.1
Cells and batteries	0.075	123.1	153.8
Brassieres	0.006	95.5	158.0
Total/average	1.000	105.4	120.3

Note: In US$ terms.
a. Not exceeding 80 percent proof.
b. Exceeding 80 percent proof.
Source: Adapted from Department of Statistics, *External Trade.*

the "small country assumption" (that is, exogenous dollar export prices) is not necessarily valid.

To sum up, the period under review is too short to observe any significant increases in exports due to the 1977 economic policy package, including devaluation. Moreover, lack of critical imported inputs (especially in the subsectors dependent on imports) and shortages of skilled labor have frustrated some of the new demand for Jamaican exports. There is evidence that the bias against exporting has been decreased to some extent. Moreover, import-substituting firms, which have experienced unusually high excess capacity owing to the depressed domestic market, have started exporting to CARICOM markets for the first time. There is no doubt that devaluation and the strict wages policy have made Jamaican exports more competitive than before. The question is whether the increase in demand can be met in the face of certain supply constraints, such as lack of imported inputs, skill shortages, and so forth. The prospects for Jamaica's nontraditional manufacturing exports are discussed in Chapter 6.

4

•-•--•

Effect of Government Policies
on the Structure of the
Manufacturing Sector

Previous chapters have shown that the system of
quantitative restrictions was by far the most significant determinant of the structure of the manufacturing sector in Jamaica. In
this chapter, some of the effects of the government's restrictive
policies on this structure are enumerated and quantified. The key
characteristics of Jamaica's manufacturing sector—high capital-intensity of most subsectors, heavy dependence on imported
inputs, high degree of industrial concentration, and low levels of
capacity utilization—are analyzed, using data from the manufacturing sector survey carried out specifically for this study.[1]

Capital-Intensity of the Subsectors

The combination of duty-free or low-duty imports of capital
goods, the choice of products designated as approved under the
incentive laws, the generous depreciation allowances, and quantitative restrictions on final products have encouraged rather
capital-intensive investment in an economy where the unem-
ployment rate averages about 25 percent.[2] Table 4-1 presents
average gross fixed capital investment per employee in the various subsectors. The contrast between subsectors oriented to-

1. The survey questionnaire is reproduced in the Appendix.
2. Firms not operating under the incentive laws have had to pay a significantly higher
level of duties on capital goods.

Table 4-1. *Fixed Assets per Employee,*
by Manufacturing Subsector, 1964 and 1978
(J$ per employee)

		1978	
Subsector	*1964*	*Sample size*	*Fixed assets*
Food	2,580.4	5	6,165.3
Beverages	7,334.1	2	22,395.4
Tobacco	2,333.8	2	692.7
Garments	n.a.	4	780.0
Footwear	} 1,011.9	2	1,442.1
Leather goods		1	2,068.8
Furniture	1,400.3	5	5,658.5
Building materials	n.a.	2	8,099.7
Paper and paper products	1,999.9	2	13,338.3
Jewelry	n.a.	2	5,680.0
Rubber and plastics	n.a.	5	10,033.5
Textiles	1,006.1	1	14,457.8
Metal products	n.a.	5	19,137.2
Chemicals	3,802.0	8	11,076.7
Pharmaceuticals and cosmetics	n.a.	4	4,272.8
Electrical appliances	n.a.	5	5,966.6
Average/total	2,715.2	55	8,605.2

n.a. Not available.

Source: For 1964, Department of Statistics, *Production Costs and Output in Large Estab-*
lishments Manufacturing (Kingston, annual issues); for 1978, the manufacturing sector
survey.

ward exports to countries outside CARICOM (cigars, garments, and leather goods) and the rest is striking in this regard. The objective of increasing employment—one of the key reasons for developing the manufacturing sector—has not been achieved. Between 1969 and 1975 the sector's value-added grew by over 20 percent in real terms, but employment increased by only 6.7 percent. Since 1975 employment has actually declined because the sector has performed so poorly.

Dependence on Imported Inputs

Given the structure that has evolved, it is hardly surprising that most of the domestic industrial activity encouraged by the various policies has had low domestic value-added and high dependence on imported inputs. Import substitution has, therefore, discouraged, rather than helped, the growth of Jamaica's manufacuring value-added. In Table 4-2, the overall import intensity is estimated at about 43 percent of total sales for 1978. If indirect imports were included, the figure would easily reach 50 percent. The figures for 1964, which are on an essentially comparable basis, point to the increasing reliance on imported inputs over time.

Degree of Industrial Concentration

As mentioned in the past chapter, the size of the import quota and the severity of quantitative restrictions was determined by the gap between domestic demand and domestic supply. Thus, where a local firm's installed capacity was adequate to meet domestic demand, it was not subject to foreign competition. Moreover, it was rare for more than one firm to be approved for manufacture of the same product. Since a potential investor could usually find substitute products that would accord him approved status, there were powerful barriers to domestic competition once the initial firm had been established. Table 4-3 shows the number of firms accounting for most or all of the domestic production of selected items. The only finished goods imported in significant amounts to complement domestic production were textiles, calculators, socks, stockings, and disinfectants. The three main subsectors that have low industrial concentration in terms of both sales and employment are garments, furniture, and footwear.

In the garment subsector the market is divided into two broad groups. The first comprises many small firms, predominantly owned by Jamaicans, employing less than ten persons, and primarily serving the domestic market, with minor portions of output being exported to CARICOM. The second group consists of a few comparatively large firms, predominantly owned by foreigners, and exclusively involved in exporting to countries outside CARICOM. In 1979 there are four firms operating under the Export Industry Encouragement Law (EIEL).

Table 4-2. *Dependence on Imports, by Manufacturing Subsector, 1964 and 1978*
(percent)

Subsector	1964	1978		Principal inputs that are imported directly
		Sample size	Dependence on imports	
Food	15.1	4	49.8	Fruit concentrates, sorbic acid, coffee, flour.
Beverages	7.2	1	39.5	Glass bottles, sugar, coffee.
Tobacco	18.6	2	64.5	Tobacco, plywood, cellophane tubes, cigar rings.
Garments	n.a.	6	37.2	Polyester knits and wovens, thread.
Footwear	} 52.0	2	19.0	Soles, vinyl, thread.
Leather goods		2	30.8	Vinyl, canvas.
Furniture	23.2	4	31.3	Fabrics, resin, yarn (lumber imported indirectly).

Building materials	n.a.	3	36.9	Latex, titanium.
Paper and paper products	60.0	3	32.5	Paper, paraffin wax.
Jewelry	n.a.	2	46.4	Silver and gold grains, stones, rubber, wax.
Rubber and plastics	n.a.	5	30.7	Chemicals, fabrics, resin, thread, tube valves, rubber.
Textiles	36.9	1	34.0	Yarns.
Metal products	64.4	4	59.7	Rolled steel, zinc, lacquer, refractory, synthetic resin.
Chemicals	35.4	5	33.2	Menthol, petrosolvent, dextrines of starch.
Pharmaceuticals and cosmetics	n.a.	3	46.8	Barks, roots, powders, aluminum tubes.
Electrical appliances	n.a.	3	39.5	Stereo components, television kits.
Average/total	18.7	50	43.4	

Note: Inputs that are imported directly as percent of total sales.
Source: Same as for Table 4-1.

Table 4-3. *Number of Firms Accounting for Most or All of Domestic Production of Selected Items*

Item	Number of firms	Percentage of domestic demand met through imports
Acids, air-conditioners, beer, carpets, condensed milk, cornmeal, detergents, filters (air and fuel), formica, galvanized sheets, grapefruit juice, jelly desserts, oleum, paper cups, polythene bags, salt, shoe polish, soap, suitcases, tires, vacuum cleaners.	1	0
Foam	2	0
Insecticides	2	55
Orange concentrate	2	5
Toasters	2	0
Automobile radios	3	0
Calculators	3	60
Disinfectants	3	30
Electrical switchgear	3	5
Socks and stockings	3	40
Textiles	3	70
Travel goods	3	15
Cigars	4	0
Frozen meats	4	0
Handbags	4	0
Radios	4	5
Adhesives	5	0
Fans	5	10
Jewelry	5	0[a]
Mens' pants	5	10
Paints	5	0
Spices	5	0
Automotive finishes	6	0
Cast iron and pipe fittings	6	20
Paper products	6	0
Shampoo	6	10
Windows	6	0
Boys' pants	7	10
Canned vegetables	7	0
Cosmetics	8	0
Garments	8[b]	10

Table 4-3 (*continued*)

Item	Number of firms	Percentage of domestic demand met through imports
Mattresses	9	0
Furniture	11[b]	0
Guava jelly	11	0
Hot pepper sauce	16	0
Footwear	21	0

a. Not including imports intended for in-bond shops.
b. Plus many small firms.
Source: Manufacturing sector survey.

In the furniture subsector, there are about ten large firms where engineering skills are emphasized. Specialized workers are employed using reasonably modern machinery. The rest of the industry consists of small producers, with emphasis on craft skill, in which a worker generally makes a product from the beginning to the end.

The footwear subsector consists roughly of two large plants (producing more than 1,500 pairs daily), four medium-size plants (500 to 1,500 pairs daily), twenty small plants (200 to 500 pairs daily), and more than 100 mini-plants (10 to 40 pairs daily).[3]

Capacity Utilization

The high capital-intensity of the sector has been accompanied by generally low utilization rates of machinery and equipment in most subsectors. The duty-free or low duty imports of capital machinery and other macroeconomic policies, together with security problems for night work, have been some of the key factors for excess capacity, apart from the Chamberlinian excess capacity resulting from oligopolistic firms producing below optimum levels.[4] There have also been certain specific causes, such as licensing agreements, which have prevented franchised

3. Information provided by Jamaica Manufacturers Association.
4. Edward H. Chamberlin, *The Theory of Monopolistic Competition* (Cambridge, Mass.: Harvard University Press, 1933).

Table 4-4. *Mean Capacity Utilization,*
by Manufacturing Subsector, 1978

Subsector	Number of firms	Utilization rate (percent)[a]	
		Mean	Standard deviation
Food processing	5	71	26
Beverages	2	50	0
Tobacco	2	62	7
Garments	5	56	16
Footwear	2	36	21
Leather products	2	54	32
Furniture	2	37	12
Building materials	2	30	3
Paper and paper products	3	65	30
Jewelry	2	35	5
Records	1	75	0
Rubber and plastics	5	73	27
Metal products	4	72	18
Chemicals	8	53	24
Pharmaceuticals and cosmetics	3	39	4
Electrical appliances	4	48	17
Total/average	52	56	24

Note: On the basis of 1.5 shifts.
a. The capacity utilization rates are simple averages of the percentage rates for individual firms. When the individual rates are weighted by output, the overall utilization rate is biased upward (to about 70 percent), because two firms in the sample (one in food processing and the other in rubber products), which account for about one-third of the total sample output, have utilization rates close to 100 percent on the basis of 1.5 shifts.
Source: Manufacturing sector survey.

firms (especially in the pharmaceuticals subsector) from making greater use of existing capacity.[5] Table 4-4 shows the mean capacity utilization rates for the subsectors and the manufacturing sector as a whole, on the basis of 1.5 shifts.

During the past few years, two factors have emerged as predominant explanations of the low capacity utilization rates: a shortage of imported raw materials and the low level of domestic demand. Of the sixty-five firms that responded to the questionnaire on this topic, forty-six (or 71 percent) included the shortage

5. This problem is discussed in the next section.

of imported raw materials as one of the main reasons for excess capacity, and most of them considered this as the key factor. Many respondents were dissatisfied with the inconveniences and delays caused by the import licensing process. The second most important factor cited was inadequate local demand. Although it is difficult to draw definitive conclusions about causality, it is worth noting that of the nine firms reporting lower capacity utilization rates in 1978 than in 1976, only one firm depended significantly on exports (export sales accounted for 45 percent of total sales), two firms sold about 75 percent of their products in the domestic market, and the rest depended completely on local sales. By contrast, of the eight firms that had higher utilization rates in 1978 than in 1976, most sold more on the foreign market than on the domestic one.[6] Partly because of the depressed domestic market and partly in response to the government's new emphasis on export promotion, several firms started exporting for the first time in 1978. Of the sixty-eight firms responding, eleven (16 percent) started exporting for the first time during 1978–79, most of them to the CARICOM area. So far, however, these export sales have not become a significant factor in affecting capacity utilization rates of firms hitherto completely dependent on local sales.

Table 4-5 provides the other main causes for excess capacity. The main local inputs in short supply were agricultural products (for use in food processing, beverage, and tobacco industries) and leather. Shortage of skilled manpower was the most important constraint for firms exporting cigars. Finally, under the category "other" causes, almost all firms referred to the power cuts that affected production in the first half of 1979.

One-shift work is the norm. As can be seen from the following figures from the survey, about 80 percent of the firms in the survey operate on the basis of a single shift.

Number of shifts	Percent of firms
1	77
2	9
3	14

6. The remaining firms either did not experience any significant change in utilization rates between the two periods or did not report their 1976 rates.

Table 4-5. *Main Causes of High Excess Capacity, 1978*

Cause	Frequency	Percentage frequency [a]
Availability of imported inputs	46	71
Inadequate local demand	27	41
Availability of local inputs	20	31
Inadequate foreign demand	13	20
Plant bottleneck	12	18
Availability of supervisory staff	8	12
Availability of skilled labor	7	11
Recent plant expansion	3	7
Other	7	11

a. Frequency as percent of total firms responding to the question.
Source: Manufacturing sector survey.

A few garment, textile, and electrical appliance firms operate two shifts. There are three shifts in some food processing industries, which produce perishables such as bread, milk, and other food products. Three-shift work is also carried out in subsectors such as metal works, chemicals, rubber, and plastics, where the high costs of shutting down and starting up appear to dominate other considerations.

The premium for overtime work is typically 50 percent for weekdays and Saturdays and 100 percent for Sundays and public holidays, although there is some variation between and within the subsectors. The premium for night shift varies between J$0.15 and J$0.25 an hour, determined generally by contracts between the unions and management. As already mentioned, however, other factors, such as problems of security for night shift workers, annul some of the incentive for this shift even when demand exists. Many firms employing three shifts said that recruiting workers for the third shift (11:00 PM to 7:00 AM) was extremely difficult and that absenteeism on that shift was very high.

When firms were asked about the most advantageous way for them to expand output, about 35 percent suggested increasing the number of shifts. About 45 percent thought that increasing overtime work was a more feasible solution in view of the shortage of skilled manpower. The remaining 20 percent of the firms considered their machinery and equipment so run-down and unsuitable that any significant increase in output would require new machinery. Some of these had already applied for licenses to import this machinery.

To conclude, the long-term factors leading to the existence of excess capacity are related to the pattern of incentives provided to the firms in the past as well as to more specific factors such as crime, improper lighting, inadequate transport, and so forth, all making the use of second and third shifts impractical or unprofitable or both. Over the past few years, the shortage of imported raw materials and insufficient domestic demand have been the predominant factors.

One of the specific reasons for the existence of excess capacity in certain subsectors has been the restrictive nature of some of the licensing agreements of the so-called franchised firms, and this issue is considered in the next section.

Franchised firms[7]

One of the needs arising from the import-substitution process, discussed in Chapter 3, was for the import of related product and process technologies. This need was fulfilled by establishing subsidiaries of multinational corporations in Jamaica's industrial sector and by technology transactions by local enterprises involved in production of their own.

Table 4-6 provides the distribution of licensing agreements for 1950–76. Only seven licensing agreements took place during 1950–65, reflecting the importance of direct foreign investment as the preferred mechanism for that period. The proliferation of licensing arrangements during the late 1960s and early 1970s was partly in response to the coming of age of the indigenous entre-

---

7. Caves and Murphy define a franchise agreement as one "lasting for a definite or indefinite period of time in which the owner of a protected trademark grants to another person or firm, for some consideration, the right to operate under his trademark for the purpose of producing or distributing a product or service." See Richard Caves and William Murphy, "Franchising: Firms, Markets and Intangible Assets," *Southern Economic Journal*, vol. 42, no. 4 (April 1976).

Table 4-6. *Frequency of Licensing Agreements, 1950 to 1976*

Year	Number of agreements	Cumulative total
1950–54	0	0
1954–59	3	3
1960–64	4	7
1965–69	19	26
1970–74	21	47
1975	15	62
1976	9	71

Source: Owen Arthur, *The Commercialization of Technology in Jamaica*, 1977.

preneurial class and partly a consequence of the setting up of CARIFTA/CARICOM, which extended these agreements to the regional market.[8]

On a sectoral basis, the agreements are concentrated in the consumer goods sector, particularly in the food and beverages subsectors, and most of these provide the recipients with exclusive production rights for the CARICOM market. More than 80 percent of these licensing agreements are with firms in the United States and United Kingdom.

As in other Caribbean countries, only a small portion of the contracts make explicit mention of patents; most involve commitments by the licensee to use a trademark together with the technology supplied.[9] To that extent, the suppliers of technology were not themselves innovators, but rather entities who, "by 'cutting and taping' together bits of knowledge" have managed to commercialize modified or new products and processes.[10]

Most licensing agreements in Jamaica contain clauses that restrict sales by the licensee to certain specific markets.[11] Since

8. See Owen Arthur, *The Commercialization of Technology in Jamaica* (Georgetown: Institute of Development Studies, Guyana, 1977).

9. For 1970–76, about 99 percent of the patents were owned by foreigners.

10. Constantine V. Vaitsos, "The Process of Commercialization of Technology in the Andean Pact," in H. Radice (edited), *International Firms and Modern Imperialism* (New York: Penguin, 1975).

11. In addition, "tie-in" import restrictions may have important repercussions on the capital- and import-intensities of the manufacturing sector and may encourage overinvoicing of imports. Unfortunately, data on these are unavailable.

Table 4-7. *Restrictions on Exports, 1976*

Export restriction	Frequency	Percentage of total
Total prohibition	12	17
Limited to CARICOM	37	52
Limited to other areas	4	6
Not specified or not applicable	18	25
Total	71	100

Source: Owen Arthur, *The Commercialization of Technology in Jamaica*, 1977.

this restriction is generally accompanied by a clause granting the manufacturer exclusive rights to produce under license in the markets in question, such a restriction is an insignificant disincentive to the Jamaican licensee. The strong local and regional demand for licenses and certain trademark rights provides testimony to this belief.

Table 4-7 shows that in about 20 percent of the cases the licensees are completely prohibited from exporting to any markets, and in another 50 percent of the cases the parties to the contract agreed to restrict exports to the CARICOM market.[12]

The implication of these restrictions for exports is clear. Roughly three-quarters of the contracts preclude licensee firms from exporting to countries outside CARICOM. Put differently, of all manufactured exports (excluding sugar, molasses, petroleum products, and re-exports) of J$110 million in 1978, about J$47 million, or 43 percent, were produced by foreign-owned firms or local firms with foreign franchises.[13] Most of these firms are legally prevented from exporting to countries outside CARICOM even if they are able to do so.

A related issue is the effect of licensing restrictions on capacity utilization rates. For example, in the pharmaceuticals subsector, the considerable spare capacity is due to restrictive licensing and patent arrangements, which prevent production of items that are currently imported. Moreover, licensing agreements between

12. "Other areas" refers to Turks and Caicos and the Cayman Islands.
13. Data obtained from Exchange Control Department, Bank of Jamaica.

local pharmaceutical firms and foreign companies "tie-in" production to the purchase of imported raw materials and expensive packaging.

Some government assessment of these technology contracts is clearly warranted. Action in this area, however, should not be precipitous. Hasty action by the government could cause licensers to cancel existing contracts, since other producers in the CARICOM region would readily pick up the franchises formerly held by the Jamaican licensees. Moreover, for licensers to remove the export restrictions on Jamaican licensees, they would have to modify similar contracts that they entered into with other Caribbean and non-Caribbean parties. The question should, therefore, be dealt with by the entire region.

5

Nominal and Effective Protection

The structure of incentives, in the form of protective measures, as well as credit, tax, and price preferences, can have a significant effect on the allocation of resources among productive activities and on the bias in favor of exporting or import substitution. On the one hand, the magnitude, source, and composition of imports will be affected by measures such as ad valorem tariffs, specific duties, and surcharges, as well as import licensing, quotas, and outright import bans. On the other hand, exports may be affected by preferential treatment in certain foreign markets, may be subject to taxes, or may receive subsidies in the producing country. Indirect taxes, price controls, credit, tax, and price preferences such as the provision of credit through government agencies on preferential terms, tax exemptions, accelerated depreciation, and preferential utility or transport rates are some other potential factors that can determine the market orientation of particular industries.

Various measures are available to assess the effects of incentive measures.[1] Among these, the nominal protection coefficient (NPC) expresses the effects of protective measures on product prices. It is defined as the ratio of domestic to world market (or border) price. Although this coefficient is useful in expressing the effects of various measures on the price of a particular product, for the producer what matters is not just the price of the

1. For a discussion of these measures, see Balassa and Associates, *The Structure of Protection in Developing Countries* (Baltimore and London: The Johns Hopkins Press, 1971).

71

output but also the cost of purchased inputs. Any protection of inputs can be viewed as a tax on such inputs.

The joint effect of protective measures on output and inputs is represented by the effective protection coefficient (EPC). This coefficient measures the extent to which trade policies cause domestic value-added to diverge from the value-added that would have prevailed in the absence of such trade policies. On the one hand, domestic value-added is derived by valuing the product and its purchased inputs in domestic prices.[2] On the other hand, value-added in world market prices, or world market value-added, is obtained by valuing the product and its purchased inputs in world market (or border) prices. An EPC exceeding unity implies that, at the existing exchange rate, protective measures provide positive incentives to the activity or the firm, whereas a coefficient less than unity signifies that, on balance, protective measures discriminate against the firm or activity. A negative coefficient generally signifies a loss of foreign exchange to the national economy.

Whereas the EPC relates the effect of protective measures on the product and its inputs, the effective subsidy coefficient (ESC) expresses the combined effects of protective measures, credit, tax, and price preferences on value-added. It is derived by adjusting the EPC for the difference between actually paid taxes, interest, and prices of nontraded goods and what are considered as normal charges under these headings.

In this study, ESCs have not been calculated because it was felt that for Jamaica, these coefficients would not be significantly different from the EPC. This is so for a number of reasons. First, the two main sources of credit to the manufacturing sector on preferential terms have been the Jamaica Development Bank (JDB), which has provided low-cost credit for the import of machinery, and the Jamaica Export Credit Insurance Corporation (JECIC), which has operated pre- and post-shipment facili-

---

2. This assumption that all purchased inputs are tradeables (that is: they are actually or potentially traded on international markets) will be qualified later when nontradeables are introduced.

ties. The interest rate subsidy by the JDB was more than elimi-
nated by the heavy losses incurred by firms using this facility due
to the exchange rate adjustments of 1977 and 1978, with firms
bearing the exchange risk. Few firms used the facilities of the
JECIC, and, as mentioned in Chapter 4, the average financial value
of the preferential interest rate was of the order of no more than
0.7 percent of the f.o.b. unit value of the products exported.[3]
Second, there are no preferential transport or utility rates for the
manufacturing sector in Jamaica. Finally, as was mentioned in
Chapter 3, direct tax exemptions have been provided to firms
approved under the Industrial Incentives Law (IIL), the Export
Industries Encouragement Law (EIEL), and, since 1974, under the
CARICOM Harmonization of Fiscal Incentives. The number of
firms approved and operating under these laws has fallen considerably, however, from 246 in 1974 to 73 in 1978. In 1978 only
3 firms were approved under these laws. It follows, therefore,
that the adjustment required to move from the EPC to the ESC is
probably so insignificant that it is not worth the effort.

The EPC and NPC are calculated below, using data from the
manufacturing sector survey.

Another measure not considered in this study is the domestic
resource cost (DRC). In calculating the EPC and ESC, domestic
value-added has been expressed in market prices. Value-added in
market prices will over- or under-state the cost to the national
economy, however, if the remuneration of the factors of production in an activity exceeds (or falls short of) their opportunity
cost. To estimate the cost to the national economy, the remuneration of productive factors is expressed in terms of shadow
prices, which reflect their opportunity costs. This measure is not
derived in this study, especially in view of scarcity of relevant
data.[4]

The EPC and NPC are calculated below, using data from the
manufacturing sector survey.

3. Of the seventy-one firms responding to questions on incentives and subsidies, only
eight had used the JDB line of credit, and only six had used the JECIC facilities.
4. For a useful study, see Inter-American Development Bank, "Pilot Study on
National Accounting Parameters: Their Estimation and Use in Chile, Costa Rica, and
Jamaica" (Washington, D.C.: IDB, October 1977).

Nominal Protection

In the absence of quantitative restrictions, price controls, or prohibitive tariffs, the NPC for domestically sold products is taken to be one plus the ad valorem rate of tariff. In cases where quantitative restrictions are significant, the NPC has to be estimated through a direct price comparison. As discussed in Chapter 4, quantitative restrictions have been the key determinant of the structure of protection in Jamaica, particularly after the mid-1960s, and, therefore, the direct price comparison method has been used.

In making price comparisons, border prices for outputs were, in almost all cases, the f.o.b. prices of any given firm's exported outputs. In the few cases where a product had not been exported during 1978, the f.o.b. price of similar exports of other firms or the c.i.f. price of similar imports was used. For inputs, border price was defined with respect to whether any given input could be imported (in which case the c.i.f. price was used) or exported (in which case the f.o.b. price was used). Domestic prices for outputs were the ex-factory prices, before any intermediate taxes had been assessed on that product. For the inputs, domestic prices were the factory gate prices of any given input, including import duties and all cascading indirect taxes. In our sample, about 45 percent of the firms paid no customs duty on inputs, and of these about 55 percent additionally did not pay indirect taxes.

The estimated NPC for each firm is the weighted sum of individual coefficients of various outputs of each firm, the weights being the domestic value of each particular output. Correspondingly, the NPC of inputs for each firm is the weighted sum of the coefficients of various inputs, the weights being the domestic value of each input.

Clearly, price comparisons of the kind mentioned are subject to pitfalls, the most obvious ones being that: (a) domestically sold varieties may be cheaper and lower quality than exported varieties; (b) imported varieties may similarly be different in quality from domestically produced varieties; and (c) in some cases the size of the sample may be inadequate for calculating NPCs for subsectors. Judgment has, therefore, played a role in arriving at an average coefficient for the subsectors from high and low values.

With these caveats, Table 5-1 presents the NPCs for outputs and inputs of the subsectors in Jamaica's manufacturing sector. Some observations can be made. First, for domestic sales the nominal protection to outputs for the overall manufacturing sector is about 34 percent, ranging from about 4 percent for furniture and garments to about 87 percent for beverages. The sample for the beverages subsector, however, does not include firms producing rum and liqueurs (which are relatively efficient exporters to markets outside CARICOM) and whose inclusion would have reduced the nominal protection somewhat. Second, in general, the nominal protection on exports to CARICOM is higher than on exports to other markets, but lower than on domestic sales. This conclusion appears to be consistent with the analysis of aggregate data from other sources discussed in Chapter 3. Third, the amount of protection varies less for inputs than for outputs. Finally, for inputs, the coefficients are generally lower for exports than for domestic sales, signifying exemptions from duties and indirect taxes on inputs for exports. These results on nominal protection are interpreted later in this chapter, together with results on effective protection.

Effective Protection

For each firm, four different EPCs were calculated: for domestic sales, for CARICOM exports, for non–CARICOM exports, and for total sales (domestic and exports). This was done to help assess the magnitude of protection at different levels (that is, domestic, CARICOM, and so forth). Total sales here refers to total production during 1978 rather than actual sales, the change in stocks of finished goods being allocated between domestic sales, CARICOM exports, and other exports according to the percentage shares of these in total sales. On the inputs side, similar adjust-

Table 5-1. *Nominal Protection Coefficients for Outputs and Traded Inputs, 1978*

	Outputs			Traded inputs		
Subsector	Domestic sales	CARICOM exports	Other exports	Domestic sales	CARICOM exports	Other exports
Food processing	1.35	1.12	1.00	1.18	1.07	1.07
Beverages	1.87	0.94	1.00	1.25	1.25	1.25
Tobacco[a]	n.a.	n.a.	1.00	n.a.	n.a.	1.12
Garments	1.04	1.16	1.00	1.20	1.17	1.17
Footwear	1.34	1.15	n.a.	1.15	1.15	n.a.
Leather goods	1.33	1.25	n.a.	1.15	1.02	n.a.
Furniture	1.04	1.00	1.00	1.20	1.04	1.04
Building materials	1.51	n.a.	n.a.	1.05	n.a.	n.a.
Paper and paper products	1.50	1.22	n.a.	1.22	1.22	n.a.
Jewelry	1.20	1.00	1.00	1.25	1.00	1.00
Rubber and plastics	1.44	0.95	1.00	1.01	1.00	n.a.
Metal products	1.21	1.12	1.00	1.11	1.11	1.11
Chemicals	1.21	1.13	1.00	1.26	1.15	1.15
Pharmaceuticals and cosmetics	1.22	1.19	1.00	1.09	1.08	1.08
Electrical appliances	1.51	1.40	1.00	1.06	1.01	1.01
Overall manufacturing	1.34	1.13	1.00	1.16	1.09	1.09

n.a. Not available.
a. Both firms in the sample exported all of their cigars to non-CARICOM markets.
Source: Manufacturing sector survey.

ments for the net difference between work-in-progress at the beginning and end of 1978 could not be made because most firms could not supply this information. Calculations for those firms that did provide this information indicate that the adjustment of total consumption of tradeables for work-in-progress makes a very small difference to the values of the coefficients. The information on nontraded inputs was broken down into two components, "tradeable" (foreign exchange) and "other," the former being allocated to tradeables and the latter being made part of value-added.[5] Here, also, some firms could not provide the components of nontraded inputs (such as electricity, petroleum, administrative expenses, and so forth). In such cases, the 1964 census of large establishments was used, which contains a wealth of disaggregated cost and output information.[6] Adjustments had to be made, however, for the change in fuel prices. Depreciation was available for firms for buildings, machinery, installations, transport equipment, tools, furniture, and other items. These were decomposed into four components: tradeable, labor, duties, and other.

Although every effort was made to collect complete and consistent data for each firm, the estimates necessitated by unavailable data described above clearly imply that the results should be treated with caution.[7] They should be viewed as illustrative of the general issues relevant to the sector.

Table 5-2 presents the results on effective protection. The first three columns provide information on the percentage share of value-added in gross output (domestic plus foreign). The second column shows this ratio at domestic prices, and the third column expresses value-added in world prices. For comparison, the first column presents the value-added shares of each of the subsectors for 1964, based on almost exactly comparable classification and

5. Since inland transportation cost for imports averaged less than 1 percent of c.i.f. prices in almost all cases, these costs were ignored.

6. See Department of Statistics, *Production Costs and Output in Large Establishments Manufacturing (Provisional Report), 1964* (Kingston, 1964).

7. Apart from the initial four man-days allocated to each firm to complete the questionnaire, there were several follow-ups to obtain specific missing information, remove inconsistencies, or find the reasons for odd-looking data.

Table 5-2. *Effective Protection Coefficients for Domestic and Foreign Sales, 1978*

	Value-added share[a]			Effective protection coefficients			
Subsector	Domestic prices, 1964	Domestic prices, 1978	World prices, 1978	Domestic sales	CARICOM sales	Other exports	Total sales
Food processing	0.34	0.36	0.35	1.53	0.98	0.90	1.30
Beverages	0.40	0.55	0.19	3.19	0.64	0.85	2.95
Tobacco	0.20	0.20	0.20	n.a.	n.a.	0.65	0.65
Garments	0.44	0.61	0.62	1.02	1.27	n.a.	1.08
Footwear	0.46	0.41	0.24	1.77	1.16	n.a.	1.74
Leather goods	0.41	0.61	0.52	1.47	1.38	n.a.	1.42
Furniture	0.41	0.56	0.57	1.01	0.99	0.99	1.00
Building materials	n.a.	0.46	0.16	1.84	n.a.	n.a.	1.84
Paper and paper products	0.54	0.50	0.27	2.09	1.25	n.a.	1.84
Jewelry	n.a.	0.52	0.49	1.16	1.00	1.00	1.08
Rubber and plastics	0.40	0.39	0.21	1.89	1.14	1.00	1.49
Metal products	0.42	0.29	0.21	1.54	1.14	0.55	1.54
Chemicals	0.48	0.62	0.52	1.17	1.13	0.99	1.15
Pharmaceuticals and cosmetics	n.a.	0.67	0.52	1.48	1.40	0.99	1.45
Electrical appliances	n.a.	0.52	0.20	2.35	1.96	1.07	2.04
Average	0.38	0.40	0.32	1.68	1.19	0.90	1.50

n.a. Not available.

a. Measures the share of value-added in gross output. In the second column, both value-added and output are valued at domestic prices, whereas in the third column, value-added is at world prices.

Source: For 1964 data, Department of Statistics, *Production Costs and Output in Large Establishments Manufacturing (Provisional Report), 1964* (Kingston, 1964); for 1978, manufacturing sector survey.

concepts.[8] The next four columns provide EPCs for domestic sales, CARICOM exports, other exports, and total sales. Several observations can be made about the results.

a. The share of value-added in Jamaica's manufacturing sector in 1978 was about 32 percent in world prices and about 40 percent in domestic prices.

b. The share of value-added in world prices was particularly low for tobacco, beverages, footwear, building materials, metal products, electrical appliances, and rubber and plastics. In the rubber and plastics subsector, value-added in world prices was negative for one of the firms, signifying that the firm was spending more foreign exchange to produce the good than it would have cost to import the product. The share of value-added was above average for garments, leather goods, furniture, chemicals and pharmaceuticals, and cosmetics.[9]

c. Compared with 1964, there were no significant changes in the share of value-added, either for the manufacturing sector as a whole or for the component subsectors. Data suggest, however, some increase in the share of value-added for garments, leather goods, and furniture and chemicals and some decrease in the more energy-intensive metal products subsector.

d. For the manufacturing sector as a whole, the values of the EPCs for domestic sales, CARICOM exports, other exports, and total sales were, respectively, 1.68, 1.19, 0.90, and 1.50.

e. There was substantial variation between the subsectors, ranging (for domestic sales) from negligible protection for garments and furniture to very high protection for beverages, building materials (especially paints) rubber and plastics, and electrical appliances.

8. Derived from Department of Statistics, *Production Costs and Output in Large Establishments Manufacturing (Provisional Report), 1964.*
9. In the sample for the manufacturing sector survey, the pharmaceuticals and cosmetics subsector is dominated by cosmetics.

f. Protection on domestic sales was significantly greater than that on export sales. Within export sales, CARICOM exports were less discriminated against than were non-CARICOM exports.

Interpretation of Results

The overall picture of the manufacturing sector that emerges confirms the generally held view of a highly protected domestic market, with nominal protection on outputs amounting to about 35 percent and effective protection of about 70 percent. By contrast there is a strong bias against exporting, particularly to countries outside CARICOM. High EPCs could reflect one or more of several factors, including excess profits, high overheads, inferior technology or organization, cost penalties associated with small-scale production of local products, and "X-inefficiencies."

There is little doubt that high profits and high overheads existed in a few cases, although data on profits were understandably sparse.[10] Even in cases where the firms did provide information on profits and overheads the data should be treated with caution. As noted in Chapter 3, to set the product price, the Prices Commission collects data on input cost and imputes a 20 percent rate of return on investment, valued at replacement cost before interest (or 15 percent after interest). The relatively small staff of the Commission, however, cannot examine all the cost data carefully, and, therefore, reported production costs can contain whatever the manager wishes to call costs. Moreover, in 1978 when there was a severe foreign exchange shortage of Jamaica, the incentive to over-invoice imported inputs was great, although it is difficult to quantify. Finally, the corporate profit tax provides an additional reason for the manager of a firm to report higher costs.

An important result in Table 5-2 is the comparison of the share of value-added in domestic and world prices. The introduction

10. According to data prepared by the Income Tax Department for 1977 for the "approved" firms (based on a sample of 111 companies, 99 under IIL and 12 under EIEL), the pretax rates of return of the firms were from 40 percent to about 75 percent.

of different tax exemptions according to the level of local or regional value-added is aimed at promoting industries with substantial proportions of value-added, on the one hand, and encouraging local or regional sectoral linkages, on the other. There is, however, a notable absence of emphasis on efficiency. The result has been to inflate the level of local value-added to a point where maximum tax exemptions become justified, with no equivalent increase in the value-added at world prices. This partly explains why for the manufacturing sector as a whole, the share of value-added in gross output at world prices is about 20 percent below the comparable figure for value-added at domestic prices.[11] A brief examination of the more important subsectors reveals diverse reasons for high effective protection.

Food processing is an industry exhibiting both reasonably high effective protection and high dependence on imports. Almost all managers in the sample firms suggested that shortages of domestic agricultural inputs had forced them to import such items as fruit concentrates, in which Jamaica presumably has a comparative advantage.[12] The high dependence of the sample firms in this subsector on imports (directly imported inputs were about 50 percent of total sales) has also meant that the exchange rate adjustments during 1978 did not have a significantly favorable effect on the industry. Given the high level of domestic protection, the incentive to export is very low. Given the depressed domestic market during 1978, however, some sample firms did export during the year, subsidizing their export operations from domestic sales.

Beverages and tobacco subsectors had particular problems. In the former, one of the key technical problems that reduced

11. The CARICOM Council has adopted a new origin system, which was implemented January 1, 1979, and under which the qualifying conditions for Common Market treatment are governed by a general rule called the "BTN jump." This requires that the final products be classified under the Brussels Trade Nomenclature (BTN) heading of any of the foreign inputs used in the manufacturing or processing operation. Although this rule may prove more effective in promoting greater linkages within and between the member countries, it is difficult to see how it will help efficiency.

12. The nominal protection for orange and grapefruit concentrates was about 220 percent.

efficient use of resources was the shortage of bottles. The West Indies Glass Factory was unable to supply local demand, and firms were forced to import bottles. The result was uncertain delivery schedules and higher than usual markups by foreign suppliers. In the tobacco subsector, both the sample firms produced only for markets outside CARICOM. Production was efficient, with zero or negative protection. The largest bottleneck to expansion, however, is the shortage of skilled cigarmakers and other skilled manpower.

The garments subsector consists of two broad groups of producers. The first group comprises a large number of firms, predominantly by Jamaicans, serving primarily the domestic market, some of which are exporting minor portions of their output to CARICOM countries. The second group consists of a small number of firms, predominantly owned by foreigners (some operating out of the Kingston Free Zone), serving exclusively export markets. Almost all the firms in the sample belong to the first category, with average sales of about J$1 million in 1978, about 10 percent of which was exported to CARICOM countries. The firms were typified by small factories and product diversity, generally using from five to ten machines. Many managers suggested that the poor layout of the factories was the main reason for inefficiencies. They also reported low profitability, which was attributed to the development in recent years of a sizable number of small garment-making firms employing less than ten persons. Firms that used to subcontract work to smaller producers in the past do not do so now for fear of nurturing potential competitors.[13]

The footwear and leather goods subsectors have been developed primarily as import-substitution operations designed to serve the domestic market. Manufacturers of shoes for the local market are required to obtain most of their leather locally. They may import one square foot of leather for every three square feet purchased from the local market. The relatively high EPCs on domestic sales of these two subsectors reflect the high price of

13. Subcontracting in this subsector (and also footwear) has also been affected by the low domestic demand of the past few years.

local inputs. Managers generally expressed concern that the establishment of the State Trading Company, a subsidiary of which will have a monopoly for importing leather, could aggravate the situation by forcing them to accept inappropriate inputs purchased by the Company under government lines of credit. Like the garments subsector, footwear is very labor-intensive and is also made up of many small units, producing small pairages.[14]

In the case of metal products, economies of scale militate against efficiency. Production is characterized by low volumes and heterogeneous final products, and lack of high-skilled personnel is an important bottleneck. Nonetheless, sample firms were able to compete successfully in the CARICOM market in items such as steel pipes and tubes, metal drums, and galvanized sheets because of duty-free entry into the CARICOM market and relatively good shipping services.

The structure of the electrical appliances subsector has been determined by the government's objective of concentrating the effort in the fields of household appliances. The sample firms produce items such as fans, radios, television sets, stereo components, stoves, and so forth. In most cases, output is on a relatively small-scale, with total sales averaging about J$1 million, a quarter of which comprise exports to CARICOM markets. The subsector basically encompasses assembly-type operations, based on imported components, such as kits and components for television and stereo sets and also items such as cathode ray tubes, electron tubes, semiconductors, and so forth. For one firm in the sample, imported inputs accounted for about 70 percent of the total sales. This, together with the low duties on these inputs (nominal protection on inputs for domestic sales was about 5 percent for the sample of firms), demonstrates the potential high cost of import substitution even with seemingly modest protection.

To summarize, Jamaica's manufacturing sector is marked by high protection on domestic sales. There is little incentive to

14. "Pairages" is a term used in this subsector to describe output in terms of pairs of shoes.

export, and where the depressed domestic market has forced firms to export, export sales have been subsidized by domestic sales. The most efficient firms are geared to the export markets outside CARICOM, but there are still particular problems, such as lack of skilled manpower, which constrain supply.

6

•··•·

Prospects for
Manufactured Exports

The government's five-year development plan for
1978–82 envisages a growth rate of about 4 percent in real terms
for the manufacturing sector. To achieve this growth, high
priority is being given to increasing exports of manufactured
goods. Adequate performance in manufactured exports will depend on several, often-interrelated factors including, but not
limited to, the following.

a. The extent to which the bias against exporting is reduced.
b. The ability of the government to continue to adhere to
   macroeconomic policies such as a realistic exchange rate
   and a restrictive wages policy.
c. The availability of imported inputs for Jamaica's import-
   dependent manufacturing sector.
d. The capacity of the entrepreneurs and the government to
   resolve, or at least to circumvent, such specific problems as
   shortages of skilled personnel, inadequate linkage with
   agriculture, problems of shipping, and so forth.
e. The ability of the government to provide adequate support
   in terms of infrastructure, credit, and promotional activity
   through such useful public entities as Jamaica Export Credit Insurance Corporation (JECIC) and Jamaica National Export Corporation (JNEC).
f. The ability of the government to assure the private sector,
   which dominates manufacturing, of its commitment to a
   mixed economy and of its new emphasis on export promotion.

The bias against exporting was examined earlier. Suffice it to say here that substantial growth of manufactured exports cannot be achieved without reducing the asymmetry in profitability of domestic and foreign sales. Currently the export market is viewed as a residual market after domestic demand has been satisfied, except for such items as cigars, beverages, garments, and certain kinds of processed foods. Of the sixty-three firms involved in exporting in the sample of seventy-one firms, fifty-five (or 87 percent) indicated that they started exporting after they had previously established their domestic market. When asked about the importance of the domestic market as prerequisite for exports, forty-seven firms considered it essential, eleven considered it important, and only five regarded the domestic market to be unimportant. By far the most frequent reason given was that local sales subsidized foreign sales, because of the higher profitability of the domestic market. A significant number of firms also considered the domestic market as a testing ground for new products, especially in terms of quality and package.[1]

Within the manufactured exports sector, there has been a significant difference in performance between exports to CARICOM and exports to the rest of the world. Thus, whereas exports to CARICOM increased by about 150 percent from US$16 million in 1972 to US$40 million in 1978, exports to markets outside CARICOM remained almost unchanged over the period. Put differently, the share of CARICOM exports in total exports increased from 33 percent in 1972 to 55 percent in 1978. The attractiveness of this market derives in large measure from the relatively generous terms of the criteria of origin, the protection afforded by the Common External Tariff, and the fact that access to CARICOM requires the least adjustment by Jamaican manufacturers in promotional activity, packaging, and so forth. As an illustration of this, of the sixty-three firms in the sample involved in export-

---

1. Two other reasons mentioned, though far less frequently, were that the domestic market acts as a training ground for a pool of skilled workers who can then be used for producing for the export sector, and that domestic sales make brand names popular with Jamaicans living abroad.

ing, forty-three (or 70 percent) considered the CARICOM most promising for exports, most of them naming Trinidad and Tobago. In fact in only five of the seventeen subsectors—food processing, beverages, tobacco, furniture, and jewelry—did most of the respondents consider markets outside CARICOM (mainly the United States, the United Kingdom, and Canada) more important. The main reasons given for considering CARICOM better for exports were the preferential treatment under CARICOM rules of origin, no need for large marketing programs, boom conditions in oil-rich Trinidad and Tobago, and relatively better shipping facilities.

There is no doubt that CARICOM has benefited Jamaica's manufactured exports considerably, as evidenced by data on the increasing share of that market in total manufactured exports. Nor is there any doubt that such trade has essentially been of the trade-creating type, since exports to the Caribbean markets have consisted of relatively capital intensive or import-intensive subsectors such as metal products, paper products, electrical equipment, pharmaceuticals, and so forth, whereas exports to countries outside CARICOM have been mainly in the beverages, tobacco, and clothing subsectors. Nevertheless, the small size of the CARICOM market (population in 1978 was about 5 million) suggests that, although this market will continue to be important in the foreseeable future, longer-term expansion will have to come from other markets. Some of the expansion in CARICOM exports has been the result of the depressed domestic market, and it may well be that once the domestic market picks up, part of the CARICOM sales may be rediverted to the more profitable domestic market.[2]

Provided Jamaica pursues realistic exchange rate and income policies, the country can expect significant growth in demand from markets outside CARICOM. In fact, manufacturers and gov-

---

2. Fishlow believes that much of the improvement in exports in Brazil during 1964–67 was due to incentives provided by domestic recession, and exports began to decline once domestic demand picked up in 1967. Quoted in Anne Krueger, *Foreign Trade Regimes and Economic Development: Liberalization Attempts and Consequences* (Cambridge, Mass.: Ballinger for NBER, 1978).

ernment officials are agreed that supply constraints to production, rather than lack of external demand, will prove the principal problems in expanding exports of manufactured goods.
Moreover, apart from a few U.S. health and safety regulations
for canned foods and fruit juices, there are no nontariff barriers in
Jamaica's principal markets outside CARICOM.[3] In addition,
Jamaica could make use of the tariff preferences offered by developed countries in a variety of semimanufactured products
under the Generalized System of Preferences (GSP). Under the
current U.S. scheme, for example, 2,700 products entering from
developing countries can enter duty-free when requirements are
met for the country of origin. Similar schemes also exist in the
European Economic Community (EEC), Japan, and the Scan-
dinavian countries.[4]

As already mentioned, supply constraints could significantly
affect Jamaica's prospects for manufactured exports. Some of the
key constraints for specific industries are identified below for
subsectors in which exports to markets outside CARICOM could
expand.

Food Processing

The food processing industry in Jamaica is composed of five
parts: (a) cereal food products, like bakery and cassava products;
(b) canning and preserving of fruits and vegetables; (c) milling,
grinding, and curing of coffee, cocoa, rice, flour, and so forth; (d)
processing of meat and dairy products such as slaughtering,
poultry, condensed milk, and ice creams, and so forth; and (e)
processing of other food products, such as edible oils and fats,
sugar, confectionary, nuts, and so forth.

Food processing is one of the production processes that utilizes
Jamaica's comparative advantage. The climate is favorable for a
variety of tropical foodstuffs. Proximity to the lucrative North

---

3. In the CARICOM market, import quotas have been imposed by Guyana since 1977
(owing to that country's balance of payments problems) on Jamaica's exports to that
country of footwear, paper products, galvanized sheets, and a few other items.

4. As regards the EEC, however, preferences under the Lome Convention override,
and are more favorable than those of the Community's GSP.

American market and the present relatively low cost of labor give Jamaica a comparative advantage in the relatively labor-intensive food processing industry.

Despite this, however, the subsector faces formidable problems that inhibit a substantial increase in exports.

a. Shortage of agricultural inputs. Demand for fruit concentrates, for instance, is large in the U.S. and European markets, but the key bottleneck is lack of a reliable supply of agricultural products. At present some apple, pear, peach, and pineapple concentrates are imported, increasing the import content of juices considerably. The government is now emphasizing the production of these agricultural products under the five-year plan, but the effect will not be visible for a few years.

b. At present, plant and equipment in many firms is run down and was planned for low-volume domestic import-substitution. To that extent, the existence of excess capacity is not really a sufficient condition for export expansion.

c. Packaging costs have increased considerably in recent years.

d. In some cases, health and safety regulations in the United States (for example, for canned, low acid foods) have prevented market penetration.

e. In the United Kingdom, Jamaican products cannot compete with processed food products from Italy, South Africa, and India partly because the governments of these countries provide export subsidies on these products.

Nonetheless, prospects for the exports of these commodities are bright, particularly in the U.S. and European markets. The improvment during 1978, shown in Table 6-1, no doubt reflects the effect of the exchange rate adjustments and the diversion of sales to foreign markets because of the depressed local market.

Beverages

The main exports in the beverages subsector are rum, liqueurs, and cordials (together accounting for 92 percent of ex-

Table 6-1. *Exports of Processed Foods, 1972 to 1978*
(US$ thousands)

Year	CARICOM	Rest	Total
1972	1,426	6,200	7,626
1976	5,364	3,898	9,262
1977	4,189	2,852	7,041
1978	6,000	4,275	10,275

Source: Department of Statistics.

ports of this subsector in 1978) with small quantities of wines, beer, and soft drinks.

Prospects for rum do not appear too favorable under the present circumstances because of stiff protection in the U.S. market in favor of the Puerto Rican product, as well as quota restrictions in the EEC market.[5] The volume and value of rum exports have declined steadily over the last few years, as can be seen from Table 6-2.

Exports of liqueurs and cordials, however, have fared somewhat better, as can be seen from the table. Even in this case, the increased volume of exports has not been reflected in terms of increased U.S. dollar receipts. Cordials and liqueurs are produced by local subsidiaries of wholly owned foreign companies.[6] The local companies have gained from devaluation in the sense that they sell their product to the parent companies at a price that compensates for the higher cost of imported inputs such as empty glass bottles, sugar, and coffee. The main beneficiaries, however, have been the parent companies because they have been paying a lower price, in terms of U.S. dollars, for the products, that is, the increase in price in Jamaican dollars to the parent companies has been less than the amount of the devaluation. This decrease in price to the parent companies has been reflected in more advertising and promotion of the product by the parent companies and in lower prices to foreign consumers. Thus, although the effect on U.S. dollar receipts for the products

5. Article 2(a) of Protocol No. 7 of EEC severely restricts rum imports from Asian, Caribbean, and Pacific countries into the market.
6. The world-famous "Tia Maria" was bought from local owners in 1957.

Table 6-2. *Exports of Rum, Liqueurs, and Cordials, 1975 to 1978*

	Rum		Liqueurs and cordials	
Year	Quantity (proof gallons)	Value (US$)	Quantity (proof gallons)	Value (US$)
1975	2,511,498	6,382,093	302,462	2,076,458
1976	2,215,008	6,579,494	881,868	7,873,804
1977	2,179,463	5,510,504	966,967	8,325,744
1978	1,872,355	5,017,761	1,009,985	7,665,510

Source: JNEC and the Department of Statistics.

is not immediately obvious because of devaluation, longer-term export competitiveness of the products has, almost certainly, been enhanced.

The companies would prefer to sell more in bulk rather than in bottled form because in some markets, such as Mexico, there are import restrictions on bottled beverages but not on bulk form; because the United States has different rates of duty for bottled and in-bulk beverages; and because particularly for the European market, transport will be substantially easier and cheaper in bulk form. Since bottling is the most labor-intensive aspect of the activity, however, the government has not viewed the shift to bulk-selling with favor, especially because it would imply a reduction in employment in the subsector.

Cigars

Four firms produce almost all of Jamaica's cigars, 90 percent of which are then exported. Between 1973 and 1978 export volume increased by about 70 percent and export value (in US$) by 110 percent (Table 6-3).

By far the most important market is the United States, and there are indications that the share of this market has increased from 76 percent of total (by volume) in 1973 to about 88 percent of total by 1978. Jamaica's share in the U.S. cigar market has declined over time, however, from about 35 percent in 1971 to about 25 percent in 1978, as shown by Figure 1.

Table 6-3. Destination of Jamaica's Cigar Exports, 1973 and 1978

	1973				1978			
Destination	Quantity (thousands)	Percentage of total	Value (US$ thousands)	Percentage of total	Quantity (thousands)	Percentage of total	Value (US$ thousands)	Percentage of total
United States	8,497	76	2,551	82	16,283	86	5,812	88
United Kingdom	1,217	11	279	9	905	5	302	5
Australia	260	2	58	2	301	2	103	2
Canada	128	1	24	1	156	1	44	1
CARICOM	341	2	50	2	183	1	68	1
Other	702	7	143	4	1,046	5	233	3
Total	11,145	100	3,105	100	18,874	100	6,562	100

Note: Data from the Department of Statistics are slightly different from those of JNEC. For 1978, JNEC data have been used.
Source: Department of Statistics, JNEC, and the Cigar Association of America.

Figure 1. *U.S. Market Share for Cigars of Jamaica and Key Competitors*

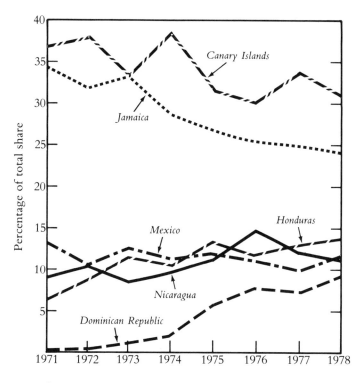

Source: JNEC.

The industry is currently suffering from two main problems. First, the dry weather conditions during 1976–78 affected the availability of local filler tobacco, forcing the firms to import this item. Thus, for the two firms in the sample, imported inputs as percentage of gross value of output in 1978 was about 65 percent, and domestic value-added (at world prices) as percentage of gross output was about 20 percent. Second, there is a general shortage of skilled cigarmakers, and this has been a significant constraint on increasing capacity utilization.

A general strategy for the subsector is that Jamaica must continue to export fine hand-made cigars rather than entering the

U.S. market with machine-made cigars. The government will, therefore, need to examine the feasibility of starting a school for cigarmakers at some point. Clearly, some filler tobacco will always have to be imported for blending purposes, but the Tobacco Industries Control Authority (TICA) should increase the output of this item. Finally, Jamaican firms should attempt to affiliate with large U.S. companies.

Prospects for Jamaica's cigar exports appear bright, assuming that Cuban cigars will continue to be unavailable in the U.S. market in the foreseeable future. The political unrest in Nicaragua clearly benefited Jamaican cigar exporters. Although the total consumption of large cigars in the United States has been declining steadily, the consumption of imported expensive cigars has increased. Thus in 1978 the consumption of "premium" cigars (with retail prices of more than US$0.50 in 1978) was US$114.5 million, an increase in nominal value of about 23 percent over the 1977 level.[7] Moreover, TICA has been getting better yields per acre recently, owing to better husbandry and the use of chemicals and new techniques.[8] On this basis, it would be reasonable to assume that the value of Jamaica's cigar exports would double to over US$15 million by 1985, compared with the 1979 level of just over US$7 million.

Garments

As mentioned earlier, the garments subsector in Jamaica is essentially dualistic. One part of it has developed on the basis of many small plants, predominantly owned by Jamaicans, with from five to ten machines, and catering to the local market with small amounts (about 10 percent) exported to CARICOM countries. The second part consists of a few firms, mostly owned by foreigners (some operating out of the Kingston Free Zone), and serving exclusively foreign markets. In the latter group exports consist primarily of garments assembled from imported fabric

---

7. Cigar Association of America, Washington, D.C.
8. Yield per acre in 1979 averaged 1,600 pounds per acre compared with 1,000 to 1,200 pounds per acre in the past.

pieces which have already been cut to size and are merely sewn together. Commonly referred to as 807 operations, after item 807.00 of the U.S. tariff schedule under which they enter the United States, such firms generally have very labor-intensive activities and are generally "footloose." For the first group, the key constraints have been the poor layout of plants, run-down machinery, and lack of skilled manpower, whereas the 807 operations are sensitive to the political climate as well as to wage costs. Although Jamaica's wage-competitiveness in garments has improved recently, labor costs are still relatively high by the standards of developing countries (Table 6-4).

As can be seen from Table 6-5, Jamaica's exports of garments declined dramatically between 1972 and 1977, mainly owing to

Table 6-4. *Labor Cost per Hour for Operators in Textile Production, in Jamaica and Selected Countries, 1976/77*
(US$)

Country	Labor cost per hour
Belgium	8.27
Netherlands	7.28
Sweden	7.20
Federal Republic of Germany	6.90
Denmark	6.68
Norway	6.21
Italy	5.15
Canada	4.92
United States	4.40
France	3.76
United Kingdom	3.14
Greece	2.23
Mexico	2.21
Turkey	1.46
Portugal	1.45
Brazil	0.92
Jamaica	0.92
Korea	0.45
Egypt	0.36
Pakistan	0.28

Source: Werner International, "Report on the Portuguese Textile and Make-up Industries" (prepared for the World Bank, June 1977).

Table 6-5. *Exports of Garments, 1972 to 1978*
(US$ thousands)

Year	CARICOM	Rest	Total
1972	1,420	8,431	9,851
1976	895	4,214	5,109
1977	669	2,287	2,956
1978	971	2,687	3,649

Note: SITC item number 84.
Source: Department of Statistics.

rising labor costs. Since that time, there are some indications of a revival, helped by the exchange rate adjustments, the wage guidelines, and the depressed domestic market. Thus in 1978, exports to markets outside CARICOM increased 17 percent, and those to CARICOM markets increased 45 percent (both in terms of U.S. dollars).

It appears that quotas in the developed countries on textiles and garments will not be a binding factor in the foreseeable future. U.S. officials state that quotas become operative for a developing country once its exports reach a level of from 30 to 40 million square yards equivalent, or about 1 percent of U.S. imports from developing countries (very roughly about US$35 million in 1976 prices).[9] In 1964, Jamaica was limited by a bilateral agreement with the United States from importing more than the equivalent of 18.5 million square yards of garments. That year Jamaica fulfilled about 85 percent of its quota. During the next ten years, however, as the quota increased gradually to about 30 million square yards equivalent in 1974, Jamaica gradually used less and less of its quota, filling only 9 percent of its 1974 allotment. Since 1974 no specific amount has been fixed. But although the 1974 U.S. quota assigned to Jamaica was twelve times greater than the country's exports in 1977, there is no guarantee that the old quota level would be retained if garment exports picked up sharply. Unfilled quotas of one country

9. See Donald Keesing, "Developing Countries' Exports of Textiles and Clothing: Perspective and Policy Choices" (Washington, D.C.: World Bank, May 1978; processed).

are generally allotted to other countries, and Jamaica may find it difficult to regain the former quota level.

The strategy for the subsector's exports that would produce the quickest results would be to revitalize the 807-type operations, with efforts being made to attract foreign firms into the subsector. Although the value-added of such an activity is not necessarily great, neither are the requirements for capital and foreign exchange, since they are provided by foreign firms. Another frequently advocated strategy for the subsector is to specialize in high quality, high-fashion garments for expensive boutiques in North America and Europe. This would entail considerable marketing and extensive contacts with American and European companies and could prove an effective long-term strategy.

Furniture

In the furniture subsector, there are about ten large firms that emphasize engineering skills, employ specialized workers, and use reasonably modern machinery. The rest of the industry consists of small producers, with emphasis on craft skill in which a worker generally makes a product from the beginning to the end.

In its present form, the furniture subsector suffers from several constraints.

a. There is a shortage of local raw materials, particularly lumber, particle board, laminates, and finishes.
b. There are quality problems. The moisture content of lumber that is not kiln-dried is at best around 12 percent. Temperate countries such as North American and European countries require a range of from 6 to 8 percent, and at present there is a shortage of kiln-drying facilities. Finishes are not up to the foreign standards in terms of materials used and their application. Moreover, the designs are not suited to export markets.
c. There is a shortage of personnel in the areas of design, industrial engineering, and quality control. On-the-job

training often tends to perpetuate current deficiencies rather than to upgrade overall skills.
d. Freight rates to Europe are high. Apparently, U.S. exporters of furniture get better freight rates to Europe than do Jamaican exporters.

Notwithstanding these drawbacks, exports of furniture have increased gradually over time, as can be seen from Table 6-6. Several Jamaican companies have entered the export market, and are becoming competitive, especially in old mahogany furniture to the United Kingdom and rattan furniture to North American markets. Part of the advantage lies in the fact that in most cases the machinery used is for general woodworking and is not specific to any particular kind of wooden product. The machinery is, therefore, quite flexible, and the capacity is responsive to demand increases. Prospects for the exports of furniture appear reasonably bright, but no significant breakthroughs can be expected in view of the constraints referred to earlier.

To summarize, prospects for Jamaica's exports depend crucially on two main factors: the extent to which the bias against exporting is reduced and the ability of the government to continue to adhere to realistic exchange rate and income policies. Once these conditions are fulfilled, substantial demand exists abroad for Jamaica's exports. There are constraints on the supply side in the form of inadequate supplies of domestic agricultural inputs, shortages of skilled manpower, poor condition of some plants and equipment, and so forth, but these are surmountable. Finally, although the CARICOM market has served Jamaica well, it has a limited size, and the country's exports will grow significantly only by expansion to markets outside CARICOM.

Table 6-6. *Exports of Furniture, 1972 to 1978*
(US$ thousands)

Year	CARICOM	Rest	Total
1972	177	150	327
1976	783	127	910
1977	1,234	363	1,597
1978	1,760	404	2,164

Source: Department of Statistics.

Appendix

•—•

Questionnaire for the Manufacturing Survey, 1978

The questionnaire requests both qualitative and quantitative information. The first part of the survey consists of about fifty questions and requires information on export markets, incentives and subsidies, pricing in the domestic market, fixed assets, capacity utilization, employment, inventory valuations, and subcontracting. The second part of the survey consists of eight tables, and requests detailed information needed for calculating the level of protection and bias against exports.

The fieldwork was carried out during June and July 1979, and about 100 firms were contacted. Of these, 71 firms completed the questionnaire either totally or partially. In addition to the initial four man-days allocated to each firm to complete the questionnaire, there were several follow-up visits to obtain missing data or to resolve inconsistencies.

A. Export Markets

1. What are your principal export markets?

	Value of exports (J$000)			
Export markets	1976	1977	1978	Projected, 1979
CARICOM				
a.				
b.				
c. Other				
Rest of the world				
a.				
b.				
c. Other				

99

2. Which of your export markets do you consider the most promising, and why?

3. Have your exports in any of the principal export markets encountered any special barriers (other than tariffs) during the past three years? In particular mention the following:

Barrier	Product affected	Export market	Date put in effect
a. Quotas			
b. "Voluntary" quotas			
c. Anti-dumping regulations			
d. Health or safety regulations			
e. Other (specify)			

4. What were the most important foreign factors, other than those listed in 3., above, that affected your exports in 1978? Please refer in particular to issues such as recession, foreign competition, competitors' export subsidies, and so forth.

5. What strategies have you followed in the past three years to deal with nontariff restrictions imposed on your exports by your principal export markets?
   a. Expansion of domestic market
   b. Change in quality
   c. Diversification to other export markets
   d. Diversification of product
   e. Other (specify)

6. If, in 1978, your f.o.b. prices for similar export items differed with respect to any of your important export markets, please provide the following:

	f.o.b. prices, 1978			
Export markets	*1*	*2*	*3*	*4*
Export items				
1.				
2.				
3.				
4.				

7. What were the main reasons for the observed f.o.b. price differences in 1978? In particular mention the following (check appropriate categories):

Reasons for f.o.b. price differences	*Main export markets affected*			
	1	*2*	*3*	*4*
a. Preferential markets				
b. Bilateral trade agreements				
c. Size of orders				
d. Cost of breaking into new markets				
e. Import quotas in foreign markets				
f. Freight and insurance				
g. Other (specify)				

8. a. In general, how did the 1978 f.o.b. prices for your exports compare with 1976? (Check appropriate answer.)

   Same as in 1976
   Lower than in 1976
   Higher than in 1976

   b. Indicate any significant differences, if any, between products or export markets.

9. If there were any cost or quality differences in similar products of your firm in 1978, between exports and domestic sales, please provide the following:

Reasons for different costs	Product			
	1	2	3	4
a. Packaging				
b. Better quality raw materials				
c. Different production process				
d. Stricter quality control				
e. Inland transport and port handling				
f. Other (specify)				
Cost and price information Estimated percentage Extra cost in 1978 Estimated f.o.b. price of domestically sold item in 1978				

10. In promoting your exports and maintaining contacts in your principal markets, which of the following methods are important? (Check appropriate categories.)

	Principal export markets			
	1	2	3	4
a. Periodic visits to customers				
b. Periodic visits of your customers to Jamaica				
c. Affiliates or subsidiaries abroad				
d. Advertising campaigns				
e. Government facilities				
f. Other (specify)				

11. In 1978 approximately how much did you spend to advertise your products in your principal export markets?

12. Did you start exporting after you had previously established your domestic market? (Check appropriate answer.)
    Yes   No

13. Indicate, in your experience, the importance of a domestic market as a prerequisite for exports. (Check appropriate answer.)
    Essential   Important   Unimportant

14. Discuss the reasons for the importance of a domestic market as a prerequisite for exports.

15. In meeting your export contracts in 1978, did you experience any large changes in freight and insurance costs? (Check appropriate answer.)
    Yes   No

16. Provide the following information on insurance and freight (i.f.) costs applicable in 1978 on your principal export items and principal export markets:

	Principal markets *(i.f. as percentage of f.o.b.)*	
Principal exports	*Least expensive*	*Most expensive*
a.		
b.		
c.		
d.		
e.		

B. Incentives or Subsidies

17. Direct tax reduction or exemption. If your firm received in 1978 any tax incentives on corporate income, please indicate the following:
    a. Nature of tax incentive, such as percentage or source of corporate income exempt from taxation.

    b. Reasons for receiving this tax incentive, such as under Industrial Incentives Law (IIL), Export Industry Encouragement Law (EIEL), and so forth.

18. Indirect tax reduction or exemption. If your firm received in 1978 any kind of indirect tax incentives, please list the taxes subject to incentives and, for each one, its nature and reason.

Indirect taxes	Nature of tax incentive	Reason for receiving tax incentives
a. Consumption duty		
b. Retail sales tax		
c. Stamp duties		
d. Tonnage tax		
e. Other (specify)		

19. Custom duty and excise reduction or exemption. If your firm received in 1978 any duty or other border tax rate reductions or exemptions, please provide the following:

   a. Imported items subject in 1978 to concessionary custom duties and the applicable duty rates.

   b. Imported items subject in 1978 to concessionary border taxes, other than custom duties (such as tonnage tax, stamp duties, and so forth) and the applicable rates.

   c. Reasons for receiving custom duty and other border tax concessions.

20. Concessionary fees for services. If your firm in 1978 used various government regulated services at concessionary rates, please list the most important of these (such as electricity, freight, and so forth), the corresponding concessionary rates your firm used in 1978, and the reason for the concessionary rates.

21. Accelerated depreciation allowance (ADA).

   a. What is the rate and value of accelerated depreciation allowance used by your firm compared with normal depreciation allowance?

   b. What are the reasons for ADA? (Industrial Incentives Law, Export Industries Encouragement Law, and so forth.)

   c. If your firm used partial ADA in 1978, please give the following:
      i. What was the book value of your depreciable assets in 1978 subject to ADA? What was this assets' percentage book value to total depreciable assets of the firm in 1978?

Depreciation of assets subject to ADA (J$000)	Depreciation of ADA assets to total depreciation (percent)

ii. What was the actual depreciation of your firm's assets subject to ADA in 1978? What was the percentage value of this depreciation to the total depreciation value for the firm in 1978?

Depreciation of assets subject to ADA (J$000)	Depreciation of ADA assets to total depreciation (percent)

22. Preferential rates of interest (PRI). If in 1978 the firm had any credits or loans outstanding at PRI, please complete the following table. (Items that could be included under "Reasons for PRI" are such things as export sales, purchase of raw materials for exports, purchase of capital goods for exports, and so forth.)

Source	Original amount	PRI	Normal rates	Reasons for PRI	Percentage in foreign exchange
a. JDB, JIDC					
b. Commercial banks					
c. Central budget					
d. Other (specify)					

23. If your firm in 1978 received any other form of government incentive or subsidy, please list the kind of incentive (such as exemption from advance deposit requirements on imported inputs, percentage reduction on tonnage tax for locally purchased inputs, and so forth) and the reasons for which they were made available.

C. Evaluation of Incentives or Subsidies

24. Evaluate the relevant importance of the various government incentives or subsidies your firm receives (or received) in assisting the firm's operation in general and the promotion of exports in particular (check appropriate categories).

Incentives or subsidies on	For firm in general			For export promotion only		
	Very impor- tant	*Impor- tant*	*Not impor- tant*	*Very impor- tant*	*Impor- tant*	*Not impor- tant*
a. Corporate taxes						
b. Consumption duty						
c. Stamp duty						
d. Tonnage tax						
e. Customs duty						
f. Excise duty						
g. Other taxes (specify)						
h. Electricity						
i. Freight						
j. ADA						
k. PRI						
l. Devaluation						
m. Others						

25. With regard to the last question, briefly explain how your firm benefited from the essential incentives or subsidies it received in promoting exports and in its overall operations. In particular, mention the effects of the devaluation in your firm's overall operations and on exports in particular.

26. Did your firm oppose the crawling peg devaluation? If so, why?

27. Have you deliberately decided at any time since 1970 not to apply for any incentives for which you are entitled?

Description of incentives	Reasons for not applying	Relevant dates
a.		
b.		
c.		
d.		
e.		

28. Describe all important domestic factors which, in your view, inhibited the growth of your exports in 1978. Feel free to suggest remedies.

D. Pricing in the Domestic Market

29. Price controls
   a. Which of your main products were subject to price controls in 1977? In 1978?

   b. How often was the price of your price-controlled product reviewed during the past three years (1976 to 1978)?

   c. What have been the grounds for the review of price controls of your products in the past three years?

30. Domestic market structure
   a. List your domestic market share for your main products as a percentage of total domestic sales in 1978.

Main products	Your share (percent)	Rest of local production (percent)	Imports (percent)
1.			
2.			
3.			
4.			
5.			

   b. How many local competitors did you have for each of your main products in 1978?

Main products	Number of main competitors
1.	
2.	
3.	
4.	
5.	

31. Distribution
   a. Indicate the methods by which your firm distributed its main products in the domestic market in 1978 as a percentage of total sales for each product.

Main products	Total sales	Over-seas	Sales to central and local govern-ment	Sales to manufac-turers	Sales to distrib-utors, whole-salers, or retailers	Sales to public	Other
1.	100.0						
2.	100.0						
3.	100.0						
4.	100.0						
5.	100.0						
6.	100.0						

   b. Indicate your sales distribution between the Kingston Metropolitan Area and the Rest of Jamaica, for domestic sales.

Main products	Percent of sales		Total domestic sales
	Kingston area	Rest	
1.			100.0
2.			100.0
3.			100.0
4.			100.0
5.			100.0

c. What means of transport did you use in 1978 to deliver
your products to the domestic and export markets?

Transport	Domestic	Export
Truck		
Railway		
Airline		
Ship		

E. Fixed Assets

32. Approximate percentages of book values in 1978 of machinery
and equipment represented by:

	Depreciated	Undepreciated
Imported (directly)		
Locally purchased		

33. Do your book values include the handling, transport, and in-
stallation charges of machinery and equipment? (Check appropriate
answer.)
    Yes   No

34. Give an estimate of the percentage of undepreciated book values
attributable to the following:

	Percentage
a. Duties and other taxes	
b. Handling and transport	
c. Installation	

35. a. What is the approximate percentage rate of import duty paid
on machinery and equipment?

b. What other taxes are paid on imported machinery and equipment? What are the rates?

c. Has your firm benefited from import duty exemptions for
imported machinery and equipment? Since which year?

d. What is the approximate percentage of book values attributable to machinery and equipment exempt from import
duties?

	Percentage
Depreciated	
Undepreciated	

36. On average, what has been the approximate percentage difference between locally purchased machinery and equipment in relation to
prices of the same or similar items available on world markets? (For
example, + 15 percent; − 10 percent.)

37. At any time during the past 10 years did you revalue your assets?
Please indicate the date(s) and the percentage revaluation involved.

F. Capacity Utilization

Causes	*Anticipated*	*Unanticipated*	*Comments*
a. Availability of local inputs			
b. Availability of imported inputs			
c. Inadequate local market demand			
d. Inadequate export market demand			
e. Availability of supervisory labor			
f. Availability of skilled labor			
g. Plant bottleneck			
h. Recent plant expansion			
i. Other			

39. With regard to the last question, indicate the nature of the
problems, steps taken to remedy them, and remaining problems.

40. If these constraints were removed, to what extent could the
capacity utilization rates be increased? (Check appropriate answer.)
Significantly   Slightly   None

41. If the increase above is not significant, what are the main reasons?

42. If you were to produce at full capacity in 1979, which cost items would have increased (decreased) more (less) than proportionately to output increases? (For example, at full capacity, output would have increased by 50 percent and labor cost by 55 percent, while depreciation would have remained unchanged.) Indicate in particular, labor costs, inventories, and depreciation. See table below.

Item	Percentage change for full capacity
a. Output	
b. Direct labor	
c. Overhead labor	
d. Inventories	
e. Depreciation	

G. Employment

43. In 1978 what were the premiums you paid for night shift and overtime work? Were they determined by law, by management/labor agreement, or by the market?

44. In 1978 what were the wage rates you paid to seasonal labor? How were they determined?

45. In 1979 what would be the most advantageous way for your firm to expand output: by adding shifts, overtime work, or increasing capacity (if plant operated at less than full capacity)? Give reasons.

H. Inventory Valuations in 1978

46. On what basis were stocks of final products valued at the beginning and end of FY 1978?

47. What was the normal percentage difference between stock and ex-factory values of final products at the beginning and end of FY 1978?

48. How was "work in progress" valued in 1978?

I. Subcontracting

49. In 1978 if your firm had subcontracted out certain processing stages for its manufacturing needs, please list the main items and the corresponding costs.

50. What is your estimate of the breakdown of these costs? Please answer with respect to the following:

	Amount or percentage
a. Materials	
b. Labor	
c. Margins	

Table 1. *Summary of Financial Data, 1976 to 1979*
(J$ thousands)

Item	1976	1977	1978	Projected, 1979
Export sales of manufacturer				
Domestic sales of manufacturer				
Total sales				
Other income				
Depreciation				
Interest paid				
Net profit or loss				
Provision for corporate taxes				
Dividends paid				
Net worth				
Fixed liabilities				
Current liabilities				
Notes and bills payable				
Inventories (total)				
Receivables				
Total assets				
Total tangible fixed assets (undepreciated book value)				
Total employment				

Notes: All balance sheet items relate to the end of each financial year. Sales figures should include all indirect taxes, if any, that the firms collect on behalf of the government.

Table 2. *Sales and Stocks, 1978*
(J$ thousand)

Item	Quantity unit, (yards, tons, etc.)	Sales in Jamaica		Sales in Jamaica to exporting firm	
		Quantity	Value[a]	Quantity	Value[a]
Principal goods manufactured					
1.					
2.					
3.					
4.					
5.					
6.					
7.					
8.					
9.					
10.					
Subtotal					
Sales of services					
1. Subcontracting of manufactured goods					
2. Other					
Subtotal					
Total					

Notes: Sales values should include all indirect taxes. Please include all items whose overall sales in 1978 exceeded 5 percent.

a. Indicate the valuation basis, such as EF (ex-factory), D (delivered), c.i.f. (cost, insurance, freight), f.o.b. (freight on board).

Direct exports to CARICOM		Direct exports to others		Total sales		Stocks of finished goods			
						Beginning		End	
Quantity	Value f.o.b./c.i.f.	Quantity	Value f.o.b./c.i.f.	Quantity	Value	Quantity	Value	Quantity	Value

Table 3. *Price Information for Some Representative Products*

Item	Product 1	Product 2	Product 3	Product 4	Product 5
Name of product					
Unit used for price information					
Sales in 1978[a]					
Domestic					
Exports					
CARICOM					
Other					
Prices in 1978					
Ex-factory prices					
Beginning					
Middle					
End					

Export prices, f.o.b. [b]
  Beginning
  Middle
  End
c.i.f. Jamaica prices of foreign
  products that are equivalent or
  similar to products sold in the
  domestic market only, in 1978
  Name
  Country of origin
  Unit used
Estimated prices, c.i.f. Jamaica, 1978
  Beginning
  Middle
  End

a. All sales are on same basis as in Table 2.
b. If f.o.b. prices for exports to CARICOM markets were different from those for other foreign markets, indicate them in parenthesis.

Table 4. Details on Material Inputs, 1978
(J$ thousands)

Material input	Quantity unit (yards, tons, etc.)	Quantity purchased	Percentage used for exports manufacturing	Total delivered cost	Stocks Beginning Quantity	Stocks Beginning Value	Stocks End Quantity	Stocks End Value
Materials and parts used directly in manufacturing								
Direct imports								
1.								
2.								
3.								
4.								
Indirect imports[a]								
1.								
2.								
3.								
4.								

Local
1.
2.
3.
4.
Subtotal

Materials and parts used
   indirectly in manufacturing
Petroleum products
Vehicles, spare parts and tires
Others
Subtotal

Supplies used for administration
   and selling

Total

Note: If possible, include all items that constitute 5 percent or more of total cost of parts and materials.
a. Bought in Jamaica from distributors, importing trade company, and so forth.

119

Table 5. Price and Indirect Tax Information on Raw Materials and Intermediate Inputs in 1976 and 1978

Item	Input 1		Input 2		Input 3		Input 4		Input 5	
	1976	1978	1976	1978	1976	1978	1976	1978	1976	1978
Name of input										
Unit used for price information (yards, tons, etc.)										
For inputs directly imported by the firm										
c.i.f. price (J$)										
Beginning										
Middle										
End										
Lending and port costs (as percentage of c.i.f.)										
Import duties[a] (as percentage of c.i.f.)										
Stamp duties (as percentage of c.i.f.)										
Other indirect taxes (as percentage of c.i.f.)										
Inland transport cost to factory										

120

Total delivered unit costs (midyear)
  For exports
  For domestic sales
For inputs purchased locally, including
  indirect imports
  Wholesale price
    Beginning
    Middle
    End
    Current (1976)
Indirect taxes (as percentage of wholesale price)
  1.
  2.
  3.
Transport of other costs
Total delivered unit cost (midyear)
Price of equivalent or similar foreign products
  Beginning
  Middle
  End
  Current (1979)

a. For inputs imported under duty drawback or other schemes, please put asterisk (★) next to numbers.

121

Table 6. *Employment, Wages, and Salaries*
(numbers and J$ thousands)

Job	1976				1977		1978	
	Employment	Wages and salaries	Fringe benefits	Total payments	Employment	Total payments	Employment	Total payments
Direct production worker								
Unskilled								
Semiskilled								
Skilled								
Part-time labor[a]								
Subtotal								
Technical personnel								
Administrative and sales personnel								
Management								
Total								

a. Show the full-time equivalent of part-time labor, on the same basis as permanent employment is reported.

Table 7. Details of Fixed Assets

Fixed asset	Depreciated or unde-preciated[a]	Book values		Book value, installed or purchased			Estimated replacement cost in 1978	Depreciation scheme[b]
		December 31, 1977	December 31, 1978	1970 and before	1970–75	1976–78		
Land	U							
	D							
Buildings	U							
	D							
Machinery and installations	U							
	D							
Buildings and installations under completion	U							
	D							
Transport equipment	U							
	D							
Tools and instruments	U							
	D							
Packaging materials	U							
	D							
Furniture and fixtures	U							
	D							
Payment against new order of fixed assets								
Total	U							
	D							

a. U = undepreciated book value; D = depreciated book value.
b. The column on depreciation should describe the predominant scheme, such as straight line or decreasing balances and the applicable rates.

Table 8. Capacity and Capacity Utilization for Main Products

Item	1		2		3		4		5		6	
	1976	1978	1976	1978	1976	1978	1976	1978	1976	1978	1976	1978
Estimated annual full capacity (in meters, tons, pairs, dozens, etc.)												
Basis for above estimate (shift hours, shifts per day, days per year)												
Number of days during the year plant not in operation due to maintenance												
Actual production (in meters, tons, etc.) or percentage of estimated annual full capacity												
Number of shifts per day, and number of days the plant was in operation (on a product-by-product basis)												

Note: In estimating annual full capacity, assume that minor debottlenecking investments can be made. Allow for seasonal supply and demand fluctuations and required maintenance time during the year.

124

Bibliography

Arthur, Owen. *The Commercialization of Technology in Jamaica.* George-town: Institute of Development Studies, Guyana, 1977.

Balassa, Bela. "Growth Strategies in Semi-Industrial Countries." *Quarterly Journal of Economics,* vol. 84 (1970).

————. "Industrial Policies in Taiwan and Korea." *Weltwirtschaftliches Archiv.,* vol. 106 (1971).

————. "Reforming the System of Incentives in Developing Countries." *World Development,* vol. 3 (1975).

Balassa, Bela and Associates. *The Structure of Protection in Developing Countries.* Baltimore and London: The Johns Hopkins Press, 1971.

Bergsman, Joel. *Brazil: Industrialization and Trade Policies.* London: Oxford University Press for OECD, 1970.

————. "Commercial Policy, Allocative Efficiency and X-Efficiency." *Quarterly Journal of Economics,* vol. 87 (1974).

Bhagwati, Jagdish N. *Foreign Trade Regimes and Economic Development: Anatomy and Consequences of Exchange Control Regimes.* Cambridge, Mass.: Ballinger for NBER, 1978.

Bhagwati, Jagdish N., and Anne O. Krueger. "Exchange Control Liberalization and Economic Development." *American Economic Review,* vol. 63 (1973).

Caves, Richard, and William Murphy. "Franchising: Firms, Markets and Intangible Assets." *Southern Economic Journal,* vol. 42, no. 4 (April 1976).

Chamberlin, Edward H. *The Theory of Monopolistic Competition.* Cambridge, Mass.: Harvard University Press, 1933.

Chen-Young, Paul. "A Study of Tax Incentives in Jamaica." *National Tax Journal,* vol. 20, no. 3 (September 1967).

Chen-Young, Paul, and Associates. "Capacity Utilization and Export Potential in the Manufacturing Sector." Study prepared for JMA, Jamaica, 1977. Processed.

Chenery, Hollis B. "Patterns of Industrial Growth." *American Economic Review*, vol. 50 (1960).

Chenery, Hollis B., and Moises Syrquin. *Patterns of Development, 1950–1970*. London: Oxford University Press for the World Bank, 1975.

Chernick, Sidney E. *The Commonwealth Caribbean*. Baltimore: The Johns Hopkins University Press for the World Bank, 1978.

Corden, William. *The Theory of Protection*. Oxford: Clarendon Press, 1971.

———. "The Structure of a Tariff System and the Effective Protection Rate." *Journal of Political Economy* (June 1966).

Department of Statistics. *Employment, Earnings, and Hours in Large Establishments*. Kingston, annual issues.

———. *External Trade*. Kingston, annual issues.

———. *Production Costs and Output in Large Establishments Manufacturing*. Kingston, annual issues.

Diaz-Alejandro, Carlos. *Foreign Trade Regimes and Economic Development: Colombia*. New York: Columbia University Press for NBER, 1976.

———. "Trade Policies and Economic Development." *International Trade and Finance*. Edited by Peter B. Kenen. Cambridge: Cambridge University Press, 1975.

Frank, Charles, K.S. Kim, and Larry E. Westphal. *Foreign Trade Regimes and Economic Development: South Korea*. New York: Columbia University Press for NBER, 1975.

Girvan, Norman. *Foreign Capital and Economic Underdevelopment in Jamaica*. Kingston: University of West Indies, 1971.

Harberger, Arnold. "Monopoly and Resource Allocation." *American Economic Review* (May 1954).

Hasan, Parvez. *Korea: Problems and Issues in a Rapidly Growing Economy*. Baltimore and London: The Johns Hopkins University Press for the World Bank, 1976.

Inter-American Development Bank. "Socioeconomic Report—Jamaica." Washington, D.C., July 1979. Processed.

———. "Pilot Study on National Accounting Parameters: Their Estimation and Use in Chile, Costa Rica, and Jamaica." Washington, D.C.: IDB, October 1977.

International Trade Center, UNCTAD/GATT. "The Fresh Fruit and Vegetables Markets in Seven European Countries," Geneva, 1968. Processed.

Jamaica Exporters' Association. "Report on Export Incentives." Kingston, November 1977.

Jamaica Manufacturers' Association. "Submission on Green Paper." Kingston, 1978.

Jefferson, Owen. *The Post-War Economic Development of Jamaica.* Kingston: University of the West Indies, 1972.

Keesing, Donald. "Outward-Looking Policies and Economic Development." *Economic Journal,* vol. 77 (1967).

———. "Developing Countries' Exports of Textiles and Clothing: Perspectives and Policy Choices." Washington, D.C.: World Bank, May 1978. Processed.

Kenen, Peter B. *International Trade and Finance: Frontiers for Research.* Cambridge, England: Cambridge University Press, 1975.

Krueger, Anne. *Foreign Trade Regimes and Economic Development: Turkey.* New York: Columbia University Press for NBER, 1974.

———. *Foreign Trade Regimes and Economic Development: Liberalization Attempts and Consequences.* Cambridge, Mass.: Ballinger for NBER, 1978.

Leith, James C. *Foreign Trade Regimes and Economic Development: Ghana.* New York: Columbia University Press for NBER, 1974.

Lewis, Stephen R. *Pakistan: Industrialization and Trade Policies.* London: Oxford University Press for OECD, 1970.

Little, Ian, Tibor Scitovsky, and Maurice Scott. *Industry and Trade in Some Developing Countries: A Comparative Study.* London: Oxford University Press for OECD, 1970.

Ministry of Industry and Commerce. "Review of Developments in Trade and Industry during the Period 1944–1954." Processed.

National Planning Agency. *A National Plan for Jamaica, 1957–1967.* Kingston: NPA, 1957.

———. "Emergency Production Plan." Kingston, 1977.

———. "Green Paper on Industrial Development Program—Jamaica, 1975–1980." Kingston, 1975.

Nelson, Richard. "The Effective Exchange Rate: "Employment and Growth in a Foreign-Exchange Constrained Economy." *Journal of Political Economy,* vol. 78 (1970).

Papageorgiou, Demetrious. "Export Promotion Policies in Less Developed Countries: The Case of Greece." Washington, D.C.: World Bank, 1977. Processed.

————. "Jamaica's Manufacturing Exports: Issues and Prospects." Washington, D.C.: World Bank, March 1978. Processed.

Pearson, Scott, Gerald Nelson, and J. Dirk Stryker. "Incentives and Comparative Advantage in Ghanaian Industry and Agriculture." Washington, D.C.: World Bank, May 1976. Processed.

Pitman, F. W. *The Development of the British West Indies, 1700–1763.* New Haven: Yale University Press, 1971.

Streeten, Paul. "Trade Strategies for Development: Some Themes for the Seventies." In *Trade Strategies for Development.* Edited by Paul Streeten. New York: John Wiley and Sons, 1973.

Thorne, Alfred P. "Size, Structure and Growth of the Economy of Jamaica." Supplement to *Social and Economic Studies,* vol. 4, no. 4 (1955).

Trade Administrator Department. "Proclamations, Rules, and Regulations." Kingston, irregular publication.

Tyler, William. *Manufactured Export Expansion and Industrialization in Brazil.* Tubingen: J. C. B. Mohr, 1976.

Vaitsos, Constantine V. "The Process of Commercialization of Technology in the Andean Pact." In *International Firms and Modern Imperialism.* Edited by H. Radice. New York: Penguin, 1975.

Werner International. "Report on the Portuguese Textile and Make-up Industries." Prepared for the World Bank. A restricted-circulation document. June 1977. Processed.

Westphal, Larry E. "Industrial Policy and Development in Korea." World Bank Staff Working Paper, no. 263. Washington, D.C.: World Bank, 1977.

————. "The Republic of Korea's Experience with Export-Led Industrial Development." *World Development,* vol. 6 (1978).

World Bank. "Caribbean Regional Study," vol. 6. A restricted-circulation document. 1975.

————. "Current Economic Position and Prospects of Jamaica." A restricted-circulation document. Washington, D.C., May 1979. Processed.

Yates, A. J. "An Analysis of the Effect of Production Process Changes on Effective Protection Estimates." *Review of Economics and Statistics* (February 1976).

World Bank Staff Occasional Papers

•—•—•••—•

(continued)

International Sales Representatives

THE UNITED KINGDOM, CONTINENTAL EUROPE, THE NEAR EAST AND
MIDDLE EAST, AND AFRICA
The Johns Hopkins University Press, Ltd., Ely House, 37
Dover Street, London WIX 4HQ, England
CANADA
University of Toronto Press, 5201 Dufferin Street,
Downsview, Ontario, M3H 5T8, Canada
AUSTRALIA AND NEW ZEALAND
Australia and New Zealand Book Co. Pty. Ltd., P.O. Box
459, Brookvale, N.S.W. 2100, Australia
INDIA
Prentice-Hall International, Inc., Englewood Cliffs, N.J. 07632,
U.S.A.
SOUTHEAST ASIA
Prentice-Hall of Southeast Asia, Pte. Ltd., 4-B, 77 Ayer Rajah
Industrial Estate, Ayer Rajah Road, Singapore 0513.
JAPAN
United Publishers Services Ltd., Shimura Building, 4-1
Kojimachi, Chiyoda-ku, Tokyo, Japan
Maruzen Co., Ltd., P.O. Box 5050, Tokyo International
100-31, Japan, and bookstores of the Maruzen Co. throughout
Japan.
LATIN AMERICA AND THE CARIBBEAN
Unilibros, 5500 Ridge Oak Drive, Austin, Texas 78731,
U.S.A.
THROUGHOUT THE REST OF THE WORLD, orders can be sent directly
to The Johns Hopkins University Press, Baltimore, Maryland
21218, U.S.A.

Published by The Johns Hopkins University Press
Baltimore and London

The full range of World Bank publications, both free and for sale, is described in the *Catalog of World Bank Publications*; the continuing research program is outlined in *World Bank Research Program: Abstracts of Current Studies*. Both booklets are updated annually; the most recent edition of each is available without charge from:

PUBLICATIONS UNIT
THE WORLD BANK
1818 H STREET, N.W.
WASHINGTON, D.C. 20433
U.S.A.